I0114152

REMAKING
THE RIGHT

REMAKING THE RIGHT

CHRIS CHAPPELEAR

Copyright © 2022 by Chris Chappelear. All rights reserved.

Library of Congress Control Number 2022912838

ISBN 979-8-9854779-7-9 (hardcover)
ISBN 979-8-9854779-8-6 (ebook)
ISBN 979-8-9854779-9-3 (paperback)

First Edition: 2022

Printed in the United States of America
10 9 8 7 6 5 4 3 2 1

TO MY DAUGHTER

TABLE OF CONTENTS

PREFACE

Traditional conservatism is dead, yet Republican elites act as if nothing is wrong. That we are in an era of peak conservatism, destined for a glorious future once we defeat the evils of the left which is always just one election away from winning. How wrong those elites are. Fully immersed in the decadence of societal rot and decay, they are blind to the truth that is staring us in the face: the Right is losing.

By any measure, the Right is losing ground in nearly every metric to the Left. Traditional nuclear families are collapsing with a decline in marriages and increases in divorce. Crime is out of control. Respect for bedrock institutions like the courts, the military, and even religion has eroded to all-time lows. Our morals are bankrupt. The culture is to the left. Education is to the left. Business is to the left. Core principles have shifted to the left. And our elites on the Right think that the answer is to cut corporate taxes once again?

No wonder we are losing.

I believe America needs a new ideology, one based in actual conservatism viewed through a populist and nationalist lens. What Donald Trump and the MAGA movement represent now is a fake populism. The rhetoric now is all about attacking their enemies, but when it comes to policy – it's the same terrible policies that the Republican establishment has supported for decades.

Except that Trump saw things more clearly at the beginning of his presidency. While it was widely derided as dark, his inaugural address American Carnage invoked a realistic portrait of America, of a nation being stripped and spat upon by elites of all parties.

Yet, there is American carnage, there is an opioid epidemic, there is a loss of our manufacturing jobs, our communities are broken, and there is a loss in our sense of America.

And our elites have no answer for any of that because they don't care about us.

When it comes to the practice of politics, I am beyond tired of the forced congeniality and the blinders people have for their own sides. If a fellow Republican is acting like a total idiot, I should be able to call them out for acting like a total idiot without being shamed for disagreeing with a total idiot.

And I don't agree with many leaders in the Republican Party that the goal should be the status quo. Have they looked at the state of our politics? The state of the world? Everything is falling apart and people are at each other's throats, even at school board meetings! And the only way the public discourse can settle itself down from this is for one side to convincingly win. Seeking compromise for the sake of compromise is pointless; there needs to be a settlement where one side wins and the other loses. It is how politics works, and has always worked.

For us to win on the right, we have to have a national vision. I heard this on a podcast somewhere, so it's not mine, but I like it: if Alexandria Ocasio-Cortez was in charge of the government, I'd know what America would look like in 10 years because she has described it so vividly and detailed in a way that it's tangible, that I would understand and any American voter would understand.

I want our candidates on the right to tell me what America will look like in 10 years, and describe it in a way that's tangible and I can see and touch, without using the words freedom, limited government, free-market, or independence. Those don't mean anything to most people, and while they're great conversations to have, they're bumper stickers, essentially.

When people have less than $1000 in their bank accounts, how are their lives going to change under the conservative plan in the next 10 years? If you can't describe it and can't detail it in an efficient way, how are voters ever going to support it or you?

In the end, our goals on the right should be to rebuild American families, restore American sovereignty, and revitalize American culture.

CHAPTER ONE

AMERICA IS FAILING

America is failing. Or at least it feels that way.

Our democracy is broken and politics feels like it's the worst it's ever been, in terms of polarization, in terms of dysfunction, or in terms of distrust. We don't trust the institutions prominent in American life, not the media, not education, not police, not even our own neighbors.

On a national level, the issues we are facing feel like late-stage empire kind of issues, particularly when we are doing things that are so self-destructive and divisive at a time when our country is in real trouble economically. Much like our society as a whole, Washington prioritizes short-term gain (boosting their chances at the next election) over making policies that will benefit our children and grandchildren. This is the end result of a godless, hyper-consumerist, hyper-liberal society.

And things are so stagnant and corrupt, that politically, nothing is happening. Frankly, I am getting a little fed up of this government. In particular, I am getting fed up of the gap between its rhetoric and its actions. More than people not believing in institutions anymore, they don't feel like they have any power. No matter what they do, no matter who they vote for, no matter what happens, they feel like they don't have any power, that the system is broken, and it's never going to change.

This is while Republican leadership decided that money is what matters most to them, so they went for Wall Street and they sold us out. Globalization, consolidation, corporate boards moving things out overseas: this has gutted our nation.

The destruction of rural and small-town America is no accident. It's a known fact that these regions breed the most conservative voters, culture, and lifestyles. As rural America dies, so too does America's conservative backbone. And Republican elites are okay with that.

Republican base voters always want better trade deals and less immigration. Yet for decades now, all the professional right has been able to give them is "we're going to cut your taxes, that's a priority, less immigration is never actually going to happen. But you still have to vote for us because we're good on abortion, and we're good on gun control." That's not enough for most people.

Most people in this country don't care about politics. They want things to work, they want to stay safe, and they want to know that the leaders they choose will do what they say and worry about politics so the people don't have to.

Conservative elites accept, fundamentally, the post-1960s settlement in American politics. This includes an enormous, unaccountable, and anti-constitutional administrative state; a permanent and bloated security state, invested in and constantly preening over endless foreign meddling; a self-serving notion of "free trade" that enriches the ruling class at the expense of the working and middle class; and a rejection of the quaint notion that a sovereign people might have the ultimate decision of who can and can't cross the border and join the political community. This ultimately means that establishment conservatives can't help but devote themselves to the conservation of leftism. They tout conservative policies that fiddle at the edges while America burns.

I don't accept that this is our lot in life, that what we have now is the best things are going to be. Authentic Americans still want to have decent lives. They want to work, worship, raise a family, and participate in public affairs without being treated as insolent upstarts in their own country. Therefore, we need a conception of a stable political regime that allows for the good life.

POLITICS IS FAILING

Republican politicians have placed so much emphasis on stupid crap that doesn't matter to the average person, they have become the worst caricatures of what the left says they are. Fox News and right-wing media are in it not just to "own the libs" but to destroy anyone that goes against whatever former President Donald Trump declares, even the insanity that is "Stop the Steal." Meanwhile, congressional Republicans are sycophant ass-kissers doing and saying whatever it takes to keep the tiny amount of power they have.

They sell their souls and whatever principles they may have had for three minutes of air-time on Tucker Carlson or Sean Hannity; United States Senators like Marco Rubio, Ted Cruz, and Josh Hawley loudly proclaim that the GOP is now the party for the workers, but when it comes to policy there isn't any change from the pro-corporate dictates from lobbyists and their donors. That's without mentioning that local and state-level Republican politicians and activists are just the same; just on a smaller, less skillful scale.

For the last 40 years, the conservative movement and Republican Party have relied upon the same slogans, the same policy prescriptions of cutting taxes, deregulation, and limited government. But what has that given us?

Our schools, the media, and the culture at large are over-run by radical left-wing progressivism. The government is larger and more inefficient than ever, and more children are born out-of-wedlock now than at any time in our history. Our infrastructure is crumbling before our eyes. And our military leadership, the one institution left that every American can agree on supporting, is more worried about imposing critical race theory than on troop readiness.

Great work there. I hope those corporate tax cuts are worth it.

The way both parties have been acting lately, I want both to lose. I'm completely sick and tired of the bullshit American politics has become.

This is not due to that bizarre notion that hyper-partisanship is tearing our country apart or that if the other side wins, democracy itself is at stake, because God forbid anyone else dare view the world differently. No, it's due to the inability of our ruling class—whether it's elected officials, career bureaucrats, academics, media personalities, corporate executives—to even understand the basics of how a country is supposed to be governed.

The conservative movement has caused what I can only describe as its own slow-moving collapse, brought on by decades of corruption and ineptitude. It coasts by on old slogans as elections are reduced to mere entertainment instead of debates about real issues, and while governance is reduced to a stagnant machine to maintain power for the political elites. Honestly, this enough for a lifelong Republican like myself to throw up my hands and exclaim, "What's the point anymore?!"

Everyone can see that the right is in shambles, even if they don't want to admit it. The elites on the right are overplaying the socialism argument because the anti-socialist narrative dovetails nicely into their desire to return the Republican Party to being the party of austerity, the party of tax cuts for the elites, and the party that attacks programs that help average Americans. It's basically an excuse to retcon the realignment that American politics is going through into an affirmation of the policies that made the GOP irrelevant to begin with.

There are too many on the right that think any concession of using government power is a concession to the left because they've been told that power will inevitably be taken over, and then all our freedoms will go away. But if you believe that, just for a second, take off your blinders and consider corporate power over your life is as detrimental as government power.

But government power is the only power the right can exercise. Education, culture, and the media are all for the left. So how does it make sense for the right not to implement a forward-looking conservative agenda and cede all power to the left? Every institution is against us today because conservatives of the past were scared to control these institutions due to the anti-big government dogma. We must wield power when we have it, or we will be crushed.

So, when I hear politicians or my friends on the right complain about the size of our government, that we shouldn't do this or that for people because of the cost, or that it interferes with the abstract idea of someone's rights; it's frustrating, to say the least.

Frankly, the size of our government is an irrelevant question; it's not shrinking anytime soon. To me, the real question is, will the government that currently exists be wielded effectively to achieve our goals, or will it be wielded by our enemies? This is what the right needs to worry about first and foremost.

All the efforts of the right need to be directed towards replacing people like Greg Abbott and Kristi Noem with leaders willing to use political power and bullying those in office to do the same. There is nothing more important, and everything else is just a distraction. Not AOC's dumb dress, foreign aid, the Afghanistan withdrawal, or whatever stupid thing Democrats are doing—all attention needs to be directed towards breaking the GOP as it currently exists.

That's because almost every multinational, every corporate, every government, they're all committed to being absolutely woke while the Republican Party has made Trump's Goldman Sachs tax cuts a hill to die on. How do you attack Democrats for basically the same policies?

An entirely different approach is required, one that explicitly rejects the idea that what the ultra-wealthy need are more tax cuts and perks. While I agree that our current government is ineffective, malevolent, and unacceptable, the problem with going the full liber-

tarian route is the solutions that ideology presents give
woke corporations a free pass for unlimited power and
control over all our lives.

It is foolish, it is naive, and it is dangerous to say
we'll just give the power to individuals, that that'll stop
Amazon and Nike from shoving critical race theory
down our throats, that Google, Facebook, and Twitter
will yield and not deplatform people who disagree with
their way of thinking.

You say you don't want to give up your individual
rights, but you already have! To corporations and all
sorts of private entities that have zero obligation or
responsibility to protect you or your rights whatsoever.

People like Candice Owens or Ben Shapiro like to
say that Trump was tackling woke corporations, but he
did nothing of the sort. He gave them massive tax cuts
without requiring them to spend the money saved in
the US. They just bought back their own stocks to arti-
ficially raise their company's stock price. Big tech and
the media are more powerful today than they were six
years ago. Thanks to Trump.

Who is going to break up big business?
Goldman Sachs?

The right-wing elites like to say that government
isn't the solution to any of your problems, that government is the problem, and that you need to rely on family
and community instead.

What a complete joke.

Families and communities are shattered, and the remnants are under siege from the left who want to destroy the nuclear family and the right-wing liberals who want atomized individuals free from relying on others to the point of not being concerned about others in their communities.

This libertarian point of view contains the seeds of progressivism and the end of the conservative way of life. As conservatives, we have to reject the selfish individualism of right-wing liberals; and in order to rebuild our communities, we have to embrace our obligations towards not just our neighbors but also to those that came before and those yet to come.

◆

When I hear people on the right talk about politics being downstream of culture, I can't help but ask why that is, or if that's even true. Why can't the dynamics between politics and culture flow in both directions, with both influencing and changing each other simultaneously? And if that's the case, then why not use political power to direct the culture?

Of course, the moment you say that to anyone in Republican politics, the cries of "socialism!" will ring out as they close their eyes and plug their ears to any thoughts or ideas other than the libertarian orthodoxy. It is entirely frustrating because if we just look at the last 20 years or so, that ideology has failed. The ideology that says forget families, forget all about that morality bullshit; what really matters is growing GDP, being able to buy cheap crap from Asia, doing whatever feels good to you, and giving people that want to destroy the traditional American way of life more tax cuts and less oversight.

There's nothing conservative about that.

It is a false dichotomy when it comes to economics on the right, which says the only alternative to free-markets and free-trade is socialism. That simply isn't true. We have to get out of this idea that everything is tax policy. Tax policy is tax policy, and you need a good one. But sending money to families with kids is not tax policy, it's a benefit that looks like social security and actually helps the people we say we care about.

Prior to free-trade, America operated under the market economy, or mercantilism. It has all the same principles of the free-market, except for the self-destructive pursuit of profit even when it's against the national interest. It shouldn't be radical to say we have some value other than profit making or that the system we have now isn't the only one that works. However, that is considered dangerous thinking because it challenges the structures of power that so many elites benefit from.

Conservative elites oppose racial hatred from the left so weakly and ineffectively that it amounts to non-opposition. Yet, when the protests and riots happened in the summer of 2020 after the murder of George Floyd and the exposure of critical race theory in

2021, the base of the country, the ordinary person who usually doesn't get involved in politics let alone vote regularly, erupted. That scared the elites because now, the people were paying attention and could see how the elites will not say that much of what the left is saying is actually anti-white racism because our elites don't want to be called racists themselves.

This obsession with self-censorship has gotten so bad that even parking tickets are cause for cancellation by right-wing elites. The worst offenders are the writers at the *National Review* and the *Bulwark*. They view purging the Republican Party of any heterodox views that go against their Ayn Rand vision of free-market fundamentalism as just the most heroic acts they can perform. They'd rather do the job of the left in order to stay in good graces of the media and the left at their Georgetown cocktail parties; making them functionally controlled opposition.

So yes, I am beyond frustrated with people who are supposed to be on the same side. I am frustrated with candidates who are running for office that would rather be bad photocopies of Donald Trump instead of running on one message: Do what will help American families.

Tax breaks for mega-corporations? No! Tax breaks for people making under $100,000 per year? Yes! This is an extremely simple and straightforward message that will work across this country, even in Democratic-leaning areas. But is that what is happening? Of course not. They would rather complain about how the 2020 election was stolen.

But in a healthy political society, most of the time, politics is not about the fundamental questions; it's about the prudential questions. We cannot imagine we are always in a time of crisis whenever the question of rights comes up. Luckily, there are a few flickers of light amongst the right. Sometimes it is for a brief moment; others are more sustained. What is clear to me is that what we currently have cannot continue. There is no sustainability or long-term vision to our political system as it stands.

Saying you stand for limited government, that isn't enough. It's a good principle, but on the right, it's become too much a slogan where we're unwilling to use political power, even when it has been handed to us. You can't shout "limited government!" every time somebody says we want to use political power for the purpose we were given it. And if you're worried that we'll have a Soviet-style state if we don't limit government, news flash: you've done a horrible job so far.

THE FUTURE IS FAILING

I have been a registered Republican since I was old enough to vote and call myself a conservative. But am I happy about that? Not really. I hate having to associate myself with the self-absorbed, arrogant, destructive, and frankly liberal behaviors and ideology that the modern conservative movement and Republican Party stand for now. In my eyes, they represent nothing more than right-wing liberalism, a poisonous ideology that must be destroyed for the right to survive in any meaningful way.

Conservative and Republican elites don't give a damn about ordinary Americans and would sell every single one of us down the river if the only alternative was doing something, anything, that would make the lives of average Americans a little bit easier. This is not hyperbole either; that situation has played out time after time, starting with the closing of American factories and shipping those jobs overseas, all in the name of free-trade and making money.

We cannot have a country where the only value is money. You can see the sickness that brings with all these people with addictions, the spike in suicides, people who just feel like they have no meaning, no purpose, no grounding, and no community, that all the life is being sucked out of their communities.

But our political elites get so caught up in these abstractions, focused on economic growth numbers or the corporate tax rate. Instead, I want a society and a country where an average person can support a family on a single income.

I don't want any more of parents having to work in the prime of their kids' lives for over 70 hours a week, having to send them off to corporate daycare because the parents can't afford the necessities of life otherwise. If any politician considers themselves pro-family or pro-life and can't agree with me on that, then they really aren't for life or families.

Our current government sucks, no question, but the conservative and Republican elite think the answer is to have no government or decentralize it. Their reactions aren't to unite but to disunite people; so, they go for these supposed forms of removing power from government and atomizing individuals. This atomization makes us weak because they fail to realize that the basic ingredient in every kind of governance is people following leaders in order to work together. That cannot happen when a community is not working together towards a common goal.

Unlike our political elites, who apparently are anarcho-corporatists, I don't believe that using government power for conservative ends is somehow evil or an abuse of power. Government power is the only power the right is able to use anymore. Being unwilling to use the only remaining power the right is able to wield because helping people goes against your "principles" but is completely fine to use on behalf of corporations, then you forfeit your right to lead anyone.

It is that kind of hypocritical behavior that has led to a feeling of complete hopelessness that anything will get better, particularly among the Millennial generation, the generation I was born into. One of the reasons for that feeling of complete hopelessness if you're below 40 years old, is what actually has been solved in your lifetime?

My generation has seen a record booming economy in the 1990s turn into whatever we're living in now. The wars in Iraq and Afghanistan were total disasters; the government and president lied to our faces as our brothers, sisters, and friends went abroad and died in those wars. We have lived through two financial booms and crashes, once while we were entering the workforce, the other in our prime earning years, wiping people out. In recent surveys of Millennials and Gen-Z, half of the respondents said they felt down, depressed, or hopeless, with a quarter of them admitting they had thoughts of self-harm several times in the previous two weeks.

Talk about a failing society.

These are the people who are the future, the bright, shining stars, with their whole lives ahead of them. They should be excited, engaged, and optimistic about the future but instead are anxious, worried, and depressed. It's a national catastrophe.

And yet, the geriatric Boomer generation that holds our nation's political leadership on both sides of the aisle refuses to lift a finger. They refuse to retire, refuse to let go of the reins of power. It's now gotten to the point that the priorities of the younger generations are not reflected in our political system at all, and you can tell.

This is not some random, intergenerational warfare: my generation has been cut off at the knees time and time again in terms of building a stable life, getting married, and all those everyday things. What Millennials have experienced in our lifetimes is one setback after setback, one crisis after crisis. What our nation needs, what future generations need, is a government that'll work to make their lives easier.

RESTORING THE RIGHT

What I am offering in this book is another option beyond the neoliberalism that is masquerading as the One and True Conservatism™ that emphasizes individualism and what's good for big business over families and communities.

Our goals on the right shouldn't be to achieve tax cuts and deregulation for the corporations, but to rebuild American families, restore American sovereignty, and revitalize American culture. But no one on the right comes close to that. The dirty little secret is that actual Republican voters don't particularly care about the philosophical debates about the nature of the state or the economic system. They want to be safe and have stability in their lives.

What I propose is far closer to the origins of conservativism: acknowledging that hierarchy, order, and communities are the foundations of society, not radical individualism. That it's important to not waste money on frivolous programs, to not let government run our lives but know that government can be used to protect us, protect our way of life, and stand as a bulwark against corporations that would chew up and spit out our people and resources with reckless abandon for the future.

Simply put: we need to do what is good for the average American family.

Like Great Britain under Benjamin Disraeli, the remedy for America lay in the revival of a feeling of nationality, community, repudiating the utilitarian self-ishness and individualism. With this must come the restoration of true religious feeling. There must follow a series of political and economic amendments: the renewal of reverence for the state, the reinvigoration of the church, the preservation of local government, the establishment of commercial codes that take cognizance of the agricultural interest; physical improvement of the condition of the laboring people. This must be a restoration, not revolution.

And we must convince Americans that they are not forgotten, that the American nation does indeed still live, that the masters of society have a common interest with the masses of society.

The challenge is that politicians on the right tend to put things in economic terms, and gradually, the language of economics takes over every aspect until there doesn't seem like any distinction between polit-ical issues and economic issues. This has damaged the conservative position greatly because precisely what conservatives are trying to say is that there are things that are jeopardized, there are things that are at risk, because of the modern way of assigning a cost to everything, of seeing everything in economic terms, the profit and the loss dominating everything rather than those things that really matter to the spiritual and moral health of the community.

Because of this dominance of the economic question, conservatism tends to be seen simply as an apology for the free-market economy, come what may.

◆

Why is the left so effective in political and cultural change? Maybe it's because they really don't have any opposition. And perhaps the reason why they don't have any opposition is that the right is militarily opposed to introspection. The right keeps complaining that the country is going to hell but doesn't stop to think that maybe we're also part of the problem. That we keep losing because we don't seem like we want to win.

I believe that we have to reject the selfish individualism of right-wing liberals and, in order to rebuild our communities, embrace our obligations towards not just our neighbors but also to those that came before and those yet to come.

The right needs to uphold the value of individuals, but our ideology cannot be just all about that. Individuals aren't out there just doing their own thing; they're plugged into a bigger picture through strong, sound, and vibrant institutions that enrich our lives.

People need something beyond themselves to focus on—a community.

We need a restoration of the old orders of morality, religion, institutions, and virtues, and a renewal of the idea that the social contract is not just between us here and now, but with us as individuals, the unborn, and those who have come before. Our natural rights are universal truths from the Almighty and cannot be defined by mere mortals in a single document, no matter how long and comprehensive we believe it to be.

Libertarians think politics can be reduced to free and equal individuals coming together on the basis of consent. But that doesn't recognize that mutual loyalties pull tribes and nations together, leaving libertarians not understanding the problem with open immigration.

And if we continue to let ourselves be fooled by representatives who claim they will reduce taxes or burdensome regulations but then do nothing but blame others for their own ineffectiveness, then we only have ourselves to blame.

CHAPTER TWO

THE BROKEN RIGHT

For years, the American political system has mainly focused not on ideas and policies but on the machinations of the political system, obsessed with messaging, raising money, winning elections, and engaging in gimmicky short-term policy ideas geared to winning a news cycle—in short, listless parties coasting by on old slogans. And the government is reduced to a stagnant machine for maintaining power while politics becomes a vast circus for loyalty signaling and emoting.

Campaigns become meaningless shows centered around personality and identity. Political debates become a clash of symbolic stands and micro-scandals to make the other party look bad. Despite the sincere belief across America that the other side is wrecking the country with terrible policies and ideas, nothing much has actually happened at all for years. For the last two decades, little of real significance has happened in American politics outside of crisis management.

Our elected officials don't behave like beacons of enlightened reason without parties to guide them. They squabble, indulge their ambitions, elevate their own petty priorities, and fail to act. There's a tendency on the right to overplay the socialism argument because the anti-socialist narrative dovetails neatly into their desire to return to being the party of austerity, the party of tax cuts, and the party that attacks Social Security. It's simply an excuse to retcon the realignment of politics into an affirmation of the policies that made the Republican Party irrelevant to begin with.

Simply put, I believe Buckley's fusion conservatism is a complete disaster.

In their 2008, 2012, and 2020 losses — and, for that matter, in their 2010 victories — Republican candidates sought to take advantage of anti-government sentiment without having to offer a vision of what the party was for when it comes to governing. As a result, thinkers and politicians on the right failed to take advantage of that period of introspection about what their governing agenda should look like.

The American left is identified with the federal government to some extent, and the public is clearly unhappy with the federal government. But what is conservatism identified with? What are voters supposed to think of when they think of the American right? Perhaps more than at any point since the founding of the modern conservative movement, today's right needs to contemplate the question: what is conservatism?

Above all, to be a conservative is to reject abstract theory and ideology. It is to be skeptical about the inevitability of progress, and to be mindful of the risks of losing what we already enjoy. It is to know that we are not solitary individuals, but social animals who belong to families, communities, and nations. It is to believe we must cooperate as much as compete with one another.

It is to respect individuality and personal freedom, but also accept constraints on freedom and our obligations toward others. It is to understand that the culture and institutions we inherit represent knowledge and wisdom that we must preserve for future generations. It is to appreciate that we understand the world not from grand theory but from the experience of life as it is lived.

Anglo-American conservatism values freedom, yet it is dependent on firmly established moral codes. Just as capitalism cannot survive without trust, so freedom cannot last without some internalized moral order. Meanwhile the left sees the state as the only vehicle for social progress.

Conservatism is individualistic only in a legal sense, and in opposition to the state; conservatives are opposed to forced collectivism and value economic freedom, especially when it comes to private property. But conservatism is communitarian in regards to informal duties, bonds, and obligations; we don't believe in absolute freedom.

A person's rugged individualism is only rugged in regards to state overreach, not his community. Once you lose those social obligations and the institutions that bind us, then what's left exactly? Conservatism is about institutions, but its fortunes are linked in particular to those of the nuclear family, just as liberalism is linked to the individual. But that individualism is what the right has been tricked into believing is true.

What conservative elites fail to realize is that conservatism is people-based, not ideas-based. Morality, religion, solidity, property, peace, order, and manners; without these values, liberty, real liberty, has little benefit and won't last.

FAILED GOVERNANCE

When the Republican establishment talks about governance, they're talking about running government like a business. To a certain extent, that's true if we mean that the government should be fiscally responsible and be mindful of the burden it places on local businesses when they overregulate and overtax. But if you keep peeling back at the metaphor, you're eventually going to run into a situation where it's a terrible idea to run the government like a business.

The idea is a good sentiment, and on its face, it makes sense. But businesses are subject to natural market pressures, and the government, by design, is not. We don't have an alternative government waiting to swoop in. It can become irrational to force the government to behave like a business and achieve the exact same results. Governments should run like governments, and businesses should run like businesses.

Likewise, if all we ever speak of is a need to limit the terms of office, cut the pay for that service (so one can survive), or make these the kinds of jobs that most of us would find miserable, then what kind of people do you think will bother to run for office? You get what you pay for. What do you suppose the motivation of the people who seek those offices might then be?

Could it be they're too incompetent to be making a decent wage in the private sector? Could it be they're seeking power? It could be that they are good-hearted souls who are willing to put off making money for a good number of years because they want the best for our country. But I am unwilling to gamble that is the primary motivating force for most people running for office if we don't provide an adequate salary to compensate them.

This is especially true now when America is no longer a democracy or a republic, but an oligarchy where the power of a few elites and special interests rig the system against regular people and where the government is run by the wealthy and corporations, who are only looking out for themselves and not the rest of us. And as I say this, keep in mind that I'm not anti-elite. I just want us to have a better elite.

◆

At this moment in history, the Republican Party of George W. Bush and Mitt Romney — operationally for open borders and reflexive free trade, unquestioningly interventionist in foreign policy, and obsequious to the corporate aristocracy of Wall Street and Silicon Valley — is gone. Thank God. But the Republican Party is depressing its base by convincing them elections don't matter because they're stolen and they're selling a paranoid fantasy.

Yet, the establishment GOP desires to be a permanent minority party of cultural grievance committed to obstruction. When it comes to redressing cultural grievances or improving the lives of the voters who back them, they will demure, citing deficit problems or allegiance to some ideology that swears off government doing anything to help you or your life.

They fail to recognize that the rock-solid, free-market, neoliberal ideology that has taken over the GOP isn't wanted by a majority of Republican voters who hate the left's woke agenda even more. The Republican elites have adopted this neoliberal ideology, and it has led us astray, teetering to irrelevance because nothing the establishment talks about applies to the grassroots.

Similarly, Conservative Inc. and other elites on the right want to get back to arguing about "normal" politics, such as what is the correct corporate tax cut and how we can lower it further. The issues they convince ordinary people to argue about are, in reality, irrelevant ones. I'm not interested in waging old political battles; I accept that spending and government interventions are needed to regulate the immoral business practices of shady, low-class operators.

I'm not alone in this; many Americans feel angry and cheated at how the American political and economic system works. Neither Democrats nor Republicans offer anything relevant to their lives. Our current political parties have stagnated into empty institutions engaged only in office seeking and graft, fighting the same tired battles over increasingly irrelevant issues.

The Republican response to complaints hasn't always been the best. Party officials and elected officials seem to be dismissive, or in some cases, back down and acquiesce to the complaints of the Democrats. This is somewhat confusing to me since those same Republicans talk a big game in private. No matter the reason for not confronting the Democrats, we need to keep one thing in mind: they hate us anyway. So why give in to their demands? Why compromise with them when Republicans have a majority? It only emboldens Democrats and gives them a platform to spout their hate and destructiveness towards our society and America.

The best way for the right to respond is not to behave as stoic philosophers lost in thought or cowardly give into their liberal demands, but to fight back against their bullshit! Take the fight to them, no matter where it is. On the floors of the legislatures, on social media, and in statements, call out the horrible policies and duplicity of Democrats. We know what they advocate for will radically change America for the worse, so why go along with the charade that those policies have any decency or usefulness for the people of this country?

But to make compelling arguments that will change people's minds, we need to not rely on intellectual argument. Yes, have that information and work it in, but that type of argument falls flat and strikes voters as cold and unfeeling. We need to use the left's own weapon against them and find compelling, emotional arguments that will instantly grab voters' attention.

FAILED ECONOMICS

There's a push among the business community to transplant Silicon Valley into places like Nebraska or Ohio to create a Silicon Prairie, but how do you think that's going to end up? The tech industry doesn't care about the Nebraska or Ohio ways of life, and when you look at the way the tech industry lobbies, what they lobby for, or their politics, it definitely won't make our states more conservative. So why does the right even entertain the idea?

Due to the dominance of the economic question, conservatism is seen as simply a vehicle to extort the values of the free-market economy, no matter what. If there's a question about an institution, like protecting the institution of marriage or primary education, it gets viewed in economic terms instead.

Everything you hear from politicians is empty platitudes made to make you feel like they are doing something. "Rejecting critical race theory." "Protecting pro-life values." "Fighting back." All of it is bullshit.

Are they saying how they'll accomplish those things? Are they going to upend the system, which is what it's going to take? The answer is an obvious no. They're going to keep pushing the same line of tax cuts and business incentives, and nothing substantial will change except for their rhetoric.

It's funny how Conservative Inc. will call themselves "principled conservatives" when they have absolutely no convictions besides bombing the Middle East. Those with power and leadership in the conservative establishment have failed us for decades. So why should we trust that they won't continue to fail us? Or think that all of a sudden, they're on our side?

Likewise, it might be cheaper to make pharmaceuticals in China or Southeast Asia, but it's challenging to convince most Americans that it's in our national interest to do so. It does not make any sense that moving all kinds of America's industrial capacity overseas is in our national interest when communities are gutted and tens of thousands of decent, stable jobs are wiped out. It's those instances where I want the government to choose the national interest over market efficiencies.

Here's a good summary of the American system as envisioned by the Republican elites: You are "free" to destroy yourself, and you're surrounded by no shortage of vice to do it. But are you free to live a fulfilling life and do what is right? No, the system will try to stop that at every turn. We need to realize that being addicted to vice isn't liberation or freedom.

On the economic side of things, we have to acknowledge that the source of the problem isn't that immigrants are taking our jobs; it's the fact that technology and automation are pushing our economy in a direction that's harder for average Americans to get by in. However, the answer for many in Con Inc. is that we must re-educate and retrain Americans for the jobs of the future, which is complete bullshit.

As a country, we are terrible at that. Government-funded retraining of manufacturing employees in the Rust Belt has only had a success rate of 0-15% in the last 30 years. And retrain for what? Are production line workers going to learn to code? AI is already starting to do simple codes. And only 8% of jobs are in STEM, so there are not enough of those jobs there.

Then we have to face the realities of life: If you're an employer, would you rather hire a 50-year-old worker with health problems, or a 25-year-old community college graduate, who's probably cheaper, has lower expectations, and is native in technology?

The fact is, the economy works really well for a select group of people, but everybody else is getting completely screwed. The unemployment rate is a poor indicator of how the economy is doing as well. People can be underpaid, doing things they don't want to be doing, or underemployed: pre-COVID, it was called the gig economy for a reason.

The last century of neoliberalism has given America stagnant wages, a devalued currency worth 1/17th of what it was worth a hundred years ago in 1922, endless wars across the globe with no sight of peace, degradation of morality and virtue, and the slow but steady grip of authoritarianism choking the life and spirit of our people.

The economy we have is a house of cards. The GOP touts free-market fundamentalism and supply-side economics as creating an economic miracle, but the reality for ordinary Americans is one of high prices, low wages, and some of the worst inequality in the world. We cannot grow our way out of this. We have to make some hard decisions.

We simply cannot allow the rate of growth in the stock market to cover up the ineptitude of our leaders anymore.

FAILED IDEOLOGY

The main driving force of the Republican Party and conservatives is called fusion conservatism, or fusionism, which was developed as an idea in the 1950s by Frank Meyer and pushed by William F. Buckley, Jr. and the *National Review*. Fusionism's central idea was to bring together libertarians, traditionalists, and militant anti-communists in order to defeat the New Deal coalition of the Democratic Party.

Neoliberalism is the idea that free-markets and free-trade are absolute good and that we must remove all regulations from industry, bring in more cheap labor in the form of immigrants, and where the individual is the most important thing, not the community.

It crosses the divide between the left and the right sides of the political spectrum, and its development and adoption by the ruling class of America ensures that there is a particular, small group of individuals who are its most fervent supporters. On the right, it can be called classical liberalism, neoconservatism, or most commonly, libertarianism. But in reality, those are all just different names for neoliberalism.

In his book, *Remaking One Nation*, author Nick Timothy explains that liberalism is best seen as a series of concentric circles. At the core is essential liberalism—the kind of values, institutions, and norms that make liberal democracy work, such as bicameral legislatures, a free judiciary, an independent press, some rights to protect minorities from the tyranny of the majority, and a commitment to an open market economy, but not free-market fundamentalism. These elements of core liberalism are shared with conservatism.

The second circle is elite liberalism, where the members of the governing class, regardless of party, share broadly liberal views about the desirability of high immigration, multiculturalism, deregulated labor markets, privatization of public services, and so on.

The third and last circle is ultraliberalism. It expresses itself on the left as cultural liberalism, which stands for increasingly militant forms of identity politics. On the right, it shows itself as free-market fundamentalists who want to deregulate and marketize services and who think that the most important thing in life is property. Both sides may often disagree with one another, but when in power, they don't repeal what the other side has done; they simply pursue their own liberal agendas.

The ideology espoused by Barry Goldwater, pushed by William F. Buckley, Jr., *National Review*, and many more think tanks and publications today isn't conservatism; it is ultraliberalism with its false idea that individual freedom means the absence of control, rather than order in the soul.

This is a sharp contrast with individualistic Anglo-American conservatism, which values freedom too. Yet freedom depends on firmly established moral codes; just as capitalism cannot survive without trust, freedom cannot last without some internalized moral order.

◆

Libertarianism is unable to have a serious constituency behind it and is not an ideology that can answer serious questions that people are facing. Yet, the way we discuss social issues on the right is captured by libertarian thought: pro-life and pro-gun. That's the only way we talk about social issues.

Whenever it comes to anything that doesn't concern economic issues or about structures like families or the way we produce families, that's something the right never knows how to talk about. The only answers libertarians have are that they are pro-life. So, if your family is living paycheck to paycheck, then you should just get another job. There's no care for if the parents are raising their own kids or if it's a daycare raising them.

The clash between libertarianism and the wider public is that the general public has a traditional view of what the real world looks like, and they listen to libertarian politicians and elites who don't see the political reality. That's what we've had for the last 30 years; our leaders are struggling to see nations or their cohesion, they're unable to see tribes, unable to see the reality of political things because they live in a fantasy world in which everyone is an atomic free-choosing individual. Naturally, they create one blunder after another, one idiotic policy after idiotic policy because they don't know what human beings are and they're not interested in learning about reality.

Neoliberals in Republican circles overuse the words freedom and liberty as some sort of code or nod to their neoliberalism without actually saying the word. But they don't really believe in those concepts, let alone know what they actually mean. They see it as something that gives them or anyone else the right to do whatever they want to do, to do anything that makes them feel good, all the while keeping up that false facade until it goes against someone else's liberties and freedom. But that's complete crap.

The basic liberties of equality before the law, freedom of speech, expression, assembly, and so on, and the capitalist market are essential to enjoying human liberty, but they are not ends in themselves. The unrestricted individualism advocated for by neoliberals is socially destructive and must at all times be wedded to a vigilant concern for the preservation of the social order.

COHESION

I have never seen the cohesion of America as frayed as it is today. If it goes far enough, then there won't be any changes of power democratically anymore; there'll be civil war. Look at a policy like immigration. There are economic arguments about who and how many new immigrants there should be. Still, it doesn't make a difference what the economic arguments are if the country is fraying so badly that adding more immigrants will literally tear the country into pieces.

Likewise, with tradition. It is a word that has almost evaporated from the American lexicon along with honor, sanctity, and God and scripture. These are things that two generations ago were still thick in the United States, and one generation ago, they still had some kind of presence. Now they've been stuffed into private corners of America, where people bring them out when they think other people aren't looking. I can't tell you what a catastrophe this is because a nation has to have things that hold it together.

You can't have cohesion over nothing; you need to have cohesion over something shared. America has been in the business now for three generations of uprooting every traditional concept that has made this country recognizable to our ancestors and our parents. I'm talking about God and scripture, and I'm talking about nation and family, I'm talking about man and woman, I'm talking about the sacred and the honorable. These keystone concepts that held our country together have come under attack, been severely damaged, and overthrown in many cases.

In American politics, the right has sadly been operating under the impression that industrial and business interests are conservative interests. That conservatism is simply a political argument in defense of significant accumulations of private property and that expansion, centralization, and accumulation are its core tenets.

But by saying you are for limited government, you are taking away people's ability to unite under a common banner for the greater good of all. You are just the tool of the progressive left that want to destroy the American way of life and the American dream. Even then, if you limit government all of a sudden people won't act like shit? They won't be self-interested and seek to gain any personal advantage that they can?

Far from moralizing, Edmund Burke thought human beings were capable of both vice and virtue. The role of politics is to limit as much as possible the vices of greed and selfishness. It is also to encourage the social virtues of generosity, loyalty, and duty that nurture the way we live in society. Appeals to the abstract ideas of liberty and equality ring hollow. They overlook the relationships with our family, friends, or fellow citizens, which provide substance to otherwise vacuous values.

Burke rejected the possessive individualism of liberal thinking in favor of social freedom. True liberty is secured by what he called "the equality of restraint", not empty free choice. But the dominant political traditions have abandoned any sense of interpersonal solidarity. They have instead embraced the impersonal forces of collective state control and atomized market exchange that undermine society.

As much as libertarians desire it, they cannot force people to be another Solon or Cincinnatus. They cannot cure people of their flaws. And it is our economic system that incentivizes and rewards behaviors that lead to crony capitalism.

RESTORATION

Conservatism has the most to offer societies that have much worth conserving, yet run the risk of dissipating their inheritance through wrong-headed, sweeping changes or stubborn inaction. In many ways, this is America's current situation. On the one hand, some progressives champion a vision characterized by government-centered technocratic expertise, arguing that the current system is weighed down by half measures and unnecessary complications. But by doubling down on centralization and technocracy, these progressives would exacerbate the very problems that have made the system ungovernable and make them permanent.

On the other hand, there are those on the right that seek to repudiate the last 80 years of institutional development and reinvent America as a nation that rejects a substantive role for regulation or a social safety net. They want to continue having the same fights over the New Deal program to abolish it, fights that the right has lost continually over the last 80 years. Though they are often labeled as "conservatives," their ambitions, and especially their rhetoric, emphasize the need for a sharp break with many features of our current governing institutions.

So, what makes up the conservative temperament? First and foremost is humility. Conservatism starts with the premise that social practices, habits, and institutions embody the accumulated wisdom of trial-and-error experience. Conservatives doubt the ability of fallible people to overhaul this evolved social order according to their vision of how it should be. Thus, conservatives doubt the usefulness of inventiveness or cleverness for their own sake in the political realm, and indeed, they fear the bad (and sometimes tragic) consequences of devotion to abstract and noble-sounding theories.

As I said before, the goal of a conservative should not be to achieve tax cuts or deregulation. It should be to rebuild American families, restore American sovereignty, and revitalize American culture. Tax cuts, at best, may sometimes serve as a means to those ends, but they are meaningless on their own. They must be supplemented with mountains of other policies that most Republican elites aren't willing to consider even though young people don't care about small government LARPing. They care about whether or not they'll be able to raise families and worship in a country that belongs to them.

The primary obstacles to conservative dominance are those neoliberals and members of Conservative Inc., who are still trying to give the 1980s a permanent lease on life. These conservative gatekeepers are not about to risk breaking up the center-right coalition established in the Reagan era by tolerating heterodox opinions from within.

It's sad to say, but Reaganism has contributed to the decline of the U.S. in terms not only of immigration policy but also foreign policy. Under the Reagan administration, many neocons cut their teeth in the bureaucracy and embedded themselves there. Which leads me to ask, what are conservatives trying to conserve now? The old brand of conservatism has either degenerated into a defense of the liberal establishment or refuses to acknowledge or grapple with the gravity of the situation we find our nation in.

Conservatism was never supposed to be about corporatocracy; it's supposed to be about family, about tradition, faith...and all of that was pushed aside because Conservative Inc. said no, it's all about making money or radical individualism. The hyper-focus on the individual leads to wokeism. If you're only focused on the individual and say whatever someone chooses is correct, then who's to say what gender you are or that you shouldn't do that, because you have no moral or social underpinning.

Politicians and elites on the right want to get back to arguing about "normal" politics, such as what is the correct corporate tax cut and how we can lower it further. The issues they convince ordinary people to argue about are, in reality, irrelevant ones. The size of our government is a frankly irrelevant question. It's not shrinking anytime soon. So, here's the real question:

will the government that currently exists be wielded effectively to achieve our goals, or will it be wielded by our enemies?

The amount of mental gymnastics and the gas-lighting required for Republican politicians to explain how their 1980s style politics will never go away because they are the baseline and the only things that matter, is exhausting. The meanings of words are essentially rendered useless; they get twisted to fit whatever narrative you desire.

We have to disabuse ourselves of whatever notions we have of what it means to be a conservative. It is a term with such a deep history, so many intricacies woven into its very fabric, but has also been so corrupted and perverted by the supposed leaders of conservatism that the word "conservative" no longer has any meaning. It is now just a slogan used by people who oppose the revolutionary cultural forces of the left. And that's not enough.

It's not enough to simply stand athwart history, saying stop. It's not enough to seek what the left wants but at a slower pace, to yearn for a past that we cannot return to. No, being a conservative is so much more.

Being a conservative is about a shared history, a shared tradition that links us together with the past as well as the future. To not accept the vanity or excesses of human nature, but to learn from our mistakes and try to make things better, even though we all have troubling and complicated pasts. Imposing an extremist set of values on the past is wholly self-destructive for a

society. Still, we should also not be afraid to acknowledge where we went wrong, to admit our society's flaws.

America still has tremendous potential, but it can
only be used if we are willing to do what is necessary to
secure our nation and use it.

CHAPTER THREE

HOW THE RIGHT GOT HERE

The neoliberalism that's been paraded around as conservatism for the last 70 years or so, championed by William F. Buckley, Jr. and the *National Review*, by Ronald Reagan, George Will, Jonah Goldberg, Bill Kristol, George W. Bush, and yes, even by Donald Trump, has been a complete disaster not just for the right, but for America. Ask the average person what Republicans stand for, and they'll say lower taxes. But there is a tremendous cost to seeking only that policy.

The imbalance in wealth in America is a direct material cause of the failure of many things people on

the right should care about, like family formation, birth
rates, the ability to thrive in the place of your birth,
and more. But the American conservative movement
doesn't care about that; it's all about opposing the left
no matter what, even if it damages or destroys societal
institutions in the process. That's how on one side we
have the left taking over and destroying organic institutions, and on the other side we have modern conservatives also destroying institutions by arguing against
collective action. Both sides are effectively executing
a pincer move, destroying the fundamental basics of
American society.

That is why I have written this book; to do what
I can to get conservatives to snap out of their blood-
thirsty rage of destroying our society and nation. It
will take more than just returning to traditional social
conservatism; we need to embrace a right-wing populist
message to rebuild and grow families and communities
that can turn away from the woke culture of the left.

Basically, the best way to think of these ideas is as
a defense of American exceptionalism in all its forms.
Not just from a chest-thumping America is the greatest
country in the world perspective, but also a defense
of things that are distinctive about American culture,
American politics, and American society that we on the
right think are good things and are worth preserving
against what we consider ill-advised efforts at reform or
transformation.

CONSERVATIVE FOUNDATIONS

The foundation of conservatism, the real kind, lies in the recognition that humans are not half as smart as they think they are. And that social change is not necessarily a good thing; It's always possible that a change, however well-intentioned, will result in disastrous consequences that are worse than the problems the change is intended to fix. The more fixed the eyes of the would-be reformers are on appealing abstractions and the less attention they give to the lessons of history, the more catastrophic the outcome generally is.

The father of conservatism, Edmund Burke's thinking on the French Revolution differed sharply from that of continental European conservatives, in that he saw no reason to object to the right of the French people to change a system of government that was as incompetent as it was despotic. But it was the way they went about it—tearing down the existing system of government root and stem, and replacing it with a shiny new system based on flashy abstractions—that Burke found problematic. It simply didn't work.

Instead of establishing an ideal republic of liberty, equality, and fraternity, the wholesale reforms pushed through by the National Assembly plunged France into chaos, handed the nation over to a pack of homicidal fanatics, and then dropped it into the waiting hands of an egomaniacal warlord named Napoleon Bonaparte, who proceeded to conquer and remake Europe.

Burke felt that the following were two bad ideas that helped feed the collapse of revolutionary France into chaos. First, the idea that human nature is entirely a product of the social order that it exists in. According to this belief, the only reason people don't act like angels is that they live in an unjust society, and once that is replaced by a just society, everybody will behave the way the moral notions of the elites insist they should.

Second, the conviction that history moved inevitably in the direction they wanted: from superstition to reason, from tyranny to liberty, from privilege to equality, and so on. According to this belief, all the revolution had to do to bring liberty, equality, and fraternity into existence was to get rid of the old order, and voila—liberty, equality, and fraternity would pop up on cue. Where the elites insisted that history moves ever upward toward a golden age in the future, and the European conservatives who opposed them argued that history slides ever downward from a golden age in the past, Burke's thesis, and the evidence of history, implies that history has no direction at all.

Burke proposed that the existing laws and institutions of a society grew organically out of that society's history and existence and themselves embody a great deal of practical wisdom. And that's without mentioning the one feature that the abstract fantasies of would-be reformers lacked: they have been proven to work. Hence, any proposed change in the law or institutions needs to start by showing that there's a need for the change; secondly, that the proposed change is going to solve the problem it claims to solve; and finally, that the benefits of the change will outweigh its costs.

This is the foundation of our Anglo-American conservatism; not the worship of the free-market or tax cuts.

BRIEF HISTORY OF THE MODERN RIGHT

Our current political system was set up so that the social liberals were aligned with populists on the left in opposition to the social conservatives and economic libertarians on the right. This has been the way politics has existed for many decades now, since the New Deal in the 1930s for the left, while the right only really coalesced in its current form of fusion conservatism, or fusionism, in the 1950s under the guiding hand of William F. Buckley, Jr. and Frank Meyer at the *National Review*.

Fusionism, quite literally, is the fusion of libertarian economics, neoconservative war-hawkishness, and traditional social conservatism. This alliance of different ideological groups came together and built up to the Reagan era and then has come apart gradually since the George W. Bush era.

Libertarians traditionally want to conserve an America that is a commercial republic; dynamic, entrepreneurial, highly capitalistic (even by the standards of the capitalist western society), and this is something that has been true of American society since the colonial era. They want to conserve a society that is defined by a general suspicion of state power and centralized authority; defend an America that's defined by local communitarianism; a mix of civic engagement, religious practice, and participation that locates a lot of the energy of American life, a lot of the forces that bind people together at the local level, in voluntary associations.

But going back into the 19th century with Manifest Destiny, there was a vision of America as a kind of empire of liberty. This republican empire first spread liberty across the continent; then, in the 20th century, it set out into the world to maintain an imperial presence around the world to preserve and sustain democratic institutions in Asia and Western Europe rather than for exploitation and pillage. At first glance, this may not seem like a bad thing, but keep going down that road, and you end up with America intervening for humanitarian reasons when it is not in our national interest to do so.

Taken in these component parts, fusion conservatism can seem self-contradictory or like a marriage of convenience of forces that don't necessarily fit well together. An Ayn Rand reading libertarian doesn't have that much philosophically in common with a conservative evangelical Christian, or a hawkish foreign policy figure might have less in common still with either of them, and so on. But what unites these groups is that they are each defending a certain aspect of what they see as America's exceptional status among advanced Western nations. The libertarian is defending America the commercial republic; the religious conservative is defending America the extremely religious and communitarian society, and the foreign policy hawk is defending America the guarantor of the liberal order worldwide.

They see themselves united in opposition to various forces on the left that, in the name of some higher or cosmic justice, are seeking changes that conservatives think would undo what makes America exceptional. The reality is that politics has a lot more going on than just these sorts of big-picture ideas and ideological visions of what America has been and should be. Most of American politics is interest-based, with people looking for their leaders, their governments, to solve immediate problems, whether those problems are economic, social, or otherwise.

Fusionism is the idea that conservatism should be a three-legged stool, combining hawkish foreign policy, social conservatism, and libertarian economics. When it first started, very few Americans bought into that overall vision. Many Americans were willing to concede that, in the wake of the New Deal and establishing a stronger central government in the first half of the 20th century, sacrificing some of their liberty for the sake of physical and economic protection from the state was a deal worth making. As such, when the early conservatives warned about an overreaching central government, those warnings fell on deaf ears.

In 1964 came the defining moment in the early conservative movement: the capture of a major party's nomination by Barry Goldwater. Goldwater was more of a libertarian than a pre-New Deal conservative. He only won the states he did in his landslide defeat because his high-minded libertarianism ended up making excuses for segregation in the deep south. Not the most auspicious beginning to translate fusionism from the pages of the *National Review* to a real-life political project.

Then, as often happens in history, fate intervened. Across the 1960s and 1970s, the liberal order went into a period of crisis. It was a crisis of public order as crime rates soared and American cities became increasingly ungovernable. It was a social crisis with the events associated with the sexual revolution, sky-high divorce rates, even higher out-of-wedlock birth rates, and a general sense of the breakdown of the family and social disorder that fed into anxieties about crime and lawlessness.

It was a foreign policy crisis as the Vietnam era gave way to the late 1970s, when American power in the world seemed to be at a low ebb and the Soviet Union seemed to be on the march. It was an economic crisis, as the Keynesian policies of the 1940s and 1950s seemed not to be working in the face of new economic realities. Suddenly, American liberals found themselves presiding over a period of stagnation and inflation at the same time, which Keynesian economists said was impossible.

At this moment, the high-minded fusion conservative vision seemed connected with actual contemporary politics and concerns. Instead of just having an abstract vision of what America should be, fusionism found its way to an actual political program that many more people were willing to vote for. Enter the Reagan era.

It started a period of fusionist conservative ascendancy across the 1980s and into the 2000s, and conservative success. If you looked back from the year 2000, you would say that conservatives campaigned in that period promising to restore American supremacy and succeeded in that. The Cold War ended, the Berlin Wall fell, and after the Reagan and H.W. Bush administrations, America stood alone as the world's sole superpower.

Conservatives campaigned on law and order and promised to make American cities safe again. Across the 1990s, in part because of reforms launched by mayors and police chiefs with input from conservative intellectuals, crime rates fell in most American cities into the 2000s. And there was stabilization in American families after the social crisis of the 1970s and 1980s. Divorce rates came down, abortion rates came down, and teen pregnancy rates began to come down.

There was a feeling in the 1990s that religion was on the upward swing again as well. While the sexual revolution hadn't been repealed, there was a sense that America had found its way to a more socially stable position in areas related to family life. And finally, we had two successive economic booms; both were associated with neoliberal policies but with a shift towards a more free-market approach to economic policy and a shift away from the state-directed economic policy of the 1970s.

Conservatives in the year 2000 could look back and say we had arrived in a moment of crisis, we made a set of promises, and at least some of those promises were fulfilled. And in the process, we have succeeded in our higher intellectual aim, which is to preserve many things about American life that we consider worth keeping.

The problem is, like many political movements that win a series of victories, conservatism became a victim of its own success. There stopped being an apparent reason for people who weren't ideologically committed to one of its specific causes to vote for conservative politicians anymore. If you voted for Republicans because you wanted to win the Cold War, that became less of an important voting issue once the Soviet Union fell. If you voted for Republicans who promised law and order when crime rates were high, as they fell, those issues became less salient.

If you voted for Republicans who cut taxes when bracket creep and inflation seemed to be raising your taxes every year, after the 17th round of Republican-led tax cuts, suddenly tax cuts were less appealing. And you might have voted for Republicans because you felt like American society and the American family were unraveling. But once society seemed to be stabilizing in specific ways, you weren't interested in going all the way with religious conservatives on abortion or premarital sex or any other issue of the sort.

♦

So, by the early 2000s, the Republican Party and conservatives no longer had a message that connected viscerally with a lot of voters who had been pulled into the Republican tent: those predominately middle- and working-class former Democrats, who were described as Reagan Democrats in the 1980s, who had once been part of the New Deal coalition, once voted for Lyndon B. Johnson, and so on. Voters were suddenly concerned about wage stagnation, health care costs, and other issues about which the Republican Party didn't have a lot to say, in part because those answers didn't necessarily fit with the party's vision of America that it was working to preserve.

The first attempt to solve this was George W. Bush's compassionate conservatism, which was to move to the center on economic policy and, in specific ways, a little bit away from the idealized libertarian vision of American society of a very limited government by doing things like passing a big education bill to increase education funding, giving a new prescription drug benefit, and spending more on anti-poverty programs, working through churches and local organizations but still spending more money. Then there was the pitch linked to the September 11th, 2001 attacks and fear of terrorism. And the right felt, briefly, like they had recaptured the Cold War moment where suddenly there was a new foreign policy issue that would cause people to vote for them to keep America safe.

Unfortunately for the right, that all fell apart. The Iraq occupation was a disaster, and no weapons of mass destruction were found. Then the Bush economic boom turned out to be just a bubble that ended in a massive financial crisis. A crisis in which certain compassionate conservatism policies, including the Bush administration's effort to increase homeownership rates by encouraging low down-payment mortgages, turned out to have been one of the forces that led to the bubble forming in the first place. Predictably, this produced a backlash within conservatism, which we know as the Tea Party movement.

Various arguments were made, but basically, there was a limited government backlash against the Bush-era compassionate conservatism. They said we had forgotten about those ideals that we were supposed to be implementing. We forgot about limited government. We went abroad to nation-build instead of being just a shining city on a hill. Those feelings defined the Tea Party moment in American politics, where there was a sense of saying no, absolutely no to compromise of any kind. No compromise on health care. No compromise on raising the debt ceiling. No compromise, just stand firm on conservative principles.

This stance worked well in the 2010 midterms, but not so much in the 2012 presidential election, where you had Mitt Romney going around the country appealing to the spirit of the heroic entrepreneur and telling people that Barack Obama's line about how you didn't build that was this terrible affront to small businessmen everywhere.

Most Americans, not being heroic entrepreneurs or small businessmen, listened to that message and thought, "What's this guy saying? What is he offering me? I don't like everything Obama did, but at least he seems connected to my economic struggles." And so, the Republican Party lost in 2012. At this point, the party seemed to be stuck with a perpetual conflict between an establishment that wanted to make deals and a base that wanted just to invest and double down in neoliberal purity.

But that paradigm missed that there was this large swath of Republican-leaning voters who basically didn't think the party had anything to say to them on the issues of most immediate concern, but also seemed intent on betraying them on other issues. Such as the massive push after the 2012 election to pass a big immigration bill that many Republican voters, not just conservatives, opposed. But the party pushed for it anyway.

This constituency was not incredibly ideologically conservative; it wasn't exceptionally moderate either; but it was essentially looking for a champion who would come to them and say, "I understand your problems, and

I'm going to do something about them, and I don't care if the things I do aren't technically conservative." This is a big part of the story of Donald Trump's primary win. He ran a primary campaign in which he flew around to parts of the country that voted Republican but have suffered economically over the last 10 to 15 years, having lost jobs, lost population, or stagnated, and he held big rallies where he promised everyone that they would get their jobs back. And this turned out to be a very effective way of winning votes.

Trump also spent a great deal of time smashing conservative orthodoxy after conservative orthodoxy. He would say that he was going to protect Medicare and Social Security, that he'd never cut them, that he was going to make sure everyone had health care. The premise of Trump's campaign was not based on the fusionism of the 1950s and 1960s. It was not religious; it was not about defending the post-World War Two liberal order. He was about going in, taking the oil, killing the terrorists, and ensuring our NATO allies paid their fair share. The part Trump really fit best into, and even then, not terribly neatly, was his vision of enduring partnerships between business and government, but not the principles of economic libertarianism.

But the turn from conservative orthodoxy didn't matter to average voters since Trump's campaign spoke to the issues on the ground: wage stagnation, job loss, disappointment with the effects of trade deals, and globalization. The things modern conservative ideology wasn't successfully addressing. He ran his primary campaign against every element that high-minded conservative intellectuals liked to tell themselves they were defending, and he found a significant constituency within the conservative coalition that was very interested in what he had to say. After the 2016 victory, the right seemed to expel, either voluntarily or not, any person who disagreed with Donald Trump's vision for the Republican Party, which is where we continue to be stuck now.

The Trump campaign of 2016 experienced a visceral hatred for anything other than the elites' carefully cultivated ideology. What those elites misunderstood, and what Donald Trump's supporters misunderstand to this day, is that we had four years where Donald Trump governed not as an authoritarian strong-man but instead as a cartoonish version of what Mitt Romney was in 2012. His supporters overlook that and say that Trump had good instincts but bad advisors. The second part is definitely true, but I cannot help but ask, if Trump had good instincts and constantly went against them, did he really have good instincts?

The only conclusion, of course, is no.

Donald Trump may have campaigned as a populist and an agent of change, but he did not govern that way. His only real legislative accomplishment was a massive corporate tax cut and large giveaways to the top income tax brackets who predominately live in New York, DC, the Bay area, or Los Angeles and make over $300,000 per year. The white woke liberals that can't stand the majority of America.

The biggest effect of the Trump tax cuts is obvious: people who own businesses and other sources of concentrated wealth will have a lot more money, and the federal budget will have less. But the advocates of the tax cuts insisted it wasn't about letting the makers keep their hard-earned money rather than handing it over to the takers. It was about incentivizing businesses to repatriate funds and ramp up their investments, thereby increasing growth and wages.

The Congressional Research Service found that none of those secondary effects have materialized. Growth has not increased above the pre-tax-cut trend. Neither have wages. After a brief and much smaller than expected bump, repatriated corporate cash from abroad has leveled off. So far, the growth feedback from the tax cuts has made up about 5 percent of the plan's revenue loss, a mere 95 percent shy of the predictions.

The promised reshoring of jobs never materialized; in fact, offshoring of jobs increased under the Trump administration. All that talk of being for law and order? Trump fundamentally transformed America's criminal justice system to favor dangerous felons. Pardons became instruments of favoritism: a few to please Trump's supporters, but the bulk for friends, allies, and special interests. The national debt soared under Trump, as did the federal workforce. He ran on getting the government off your back, but while in office, he increased the size of government and the worst parts of it.

The 2020 campaign became totally derailed by the onset of COVID-19 in the world. What was seen as a relatively solid lead for Republicans was whittled away by inaction and confusion from Trump and congressional Republicans. As the pandemic wore on, Republicans relied more on culture war fights than any policies that the Trump administration pursued or achieved. Trumpism, the beginnings of an ideology he campaigned on in 2016, was populist and mercantilist. It was skeptical of free trade, skeptical of mass immigration, and perfectly fine with entitlement programs and big infrastructure projects. But that is no longer what MAGA or America First means. It became simply agreeing with whatever Donald Trump said.

After the Republican loss in 2020, the right felt like it was in total freefall, pulled in a thousand different directions. Partly by the Republican establishment who wanted a return to their comfort zone of fusion conservatism, but more worryingly, also by absolute grifters and charlatans who used Trump's defeat to tear at the structure of the Republican Party and destroy as much of the public's trust in the party as they could. Sidney Powell, Lin Wood, and Mike Lindell were the most visible of the skeptics who propelled conspiracy theories that Trump actually won the 2020 contest due to the hacking of ballot counting machines, ballots made from bamboo paper, and more. All of it, a total lie.

Donald Trump started to believe the conspiracies himself, likely as a coping mechanism for his loss. These conspiracies, the refusal to accept the election results, and the distrust of mail-in ballots led to both U.S. Senate seats from Georgia being won by the Democrats in the run-off election on January 5th, 2021, leaving a 50-50 tie in the U.S. Senate. And these conspiracies fueled the riots at the U.S. Capitol building on the next day, January 6th, leaving four dead.

Since leaving office, Trump has doubled down on the stolen election conspiracy theory to the point that his endorsements for the 2022 midterm elections largely depend on candidates agreeing that Trump really won in 2020, and not much else. Elsewhere, the party largely relied on the mistakes of congressional Democrats and the Biden administration to deflect from their own failures.

America First is a movement with no idea who it is, what it wants, or what it's currently doing other than repackaging the same old talking points of tax cuts and "socialism sucks!" That message probably works for the very dedicated, very online supporters of Donald Trump but doesn't reach anyone who's not already tied into that world, which is most Americans.

Rather quickly after the 2020 election, it became a common trope for Republican politicians to claim that the GOP is now the party of the working class and to start hammering the tech companies for silencing conservative voices on their platforms. All of which is highly amusing when you realize that they may be using populist talking points, but they still cling dearly to the rather destructive ideology of libertarianism.

Beyond just the hypocrisy of labeling any departure from their free-trade, free-market fundamentalist point-of-view as "socialism" while they take bailouts, tax breaks, and any other handouts they get their hands on while lobbying tooth and nail to ensure productive enterprises that employ working class people have no access to the same resources, it is ludicrous to continue to prop up an economic policy that is deeply unpopular with the general population.

◆

The conservative movement in the 1990s and 2000s was drunk with this feeling of power due to the victory over communism, and people drunk with power lose touch with reality. Our leaders forgot anything that they had ever known about how to conserve anything; they lost all interest in Edmund Burke, in traditionalism, and the details of the Anglo-American political inheritance except for a few lines that they keep quoting over and over as if it were their universal dogma.

All that interested them was economic liberalism and the rights of free and equal individuals. Abandoning conservatism, the conservative elite became a revolutionary movement, declaring that universal liberal empire was the historical purpose of America since its founding, and they set out on a mission to uproot it all. For generations now, we've watched as these neoliberals waste their energy, political capital, financial resources, and the lives of hundreds of thousands of service members and civilians. All of this in the vain, prideful, and ultimately fatal conceit that their very own minds had unlocked the secret to bringing perpetual peace and prosperity to the world.

Now, we live in the wreckage brought about by that fatal conceit. With its own hands, America has built up China as a genuine rival and threat. The Middle East has been set to the flame by America with nothing to show but humiliation. The American industrial heartland has shuttered its factories, the country has been flooded with porn and drugs, and our economy has been given over to people who openly aspire to expand their corrupt, witless rule over all mankind. America has abandoned any thought of balancing its budget or paying its debts. Its borders have been effectively dissolved, and our educators have determined that only Marxism and libertarianism are the only legitimate worldviews to teach and that no conservative scholar will be hired again.

Like I said earlier, great job there.

CHAPTER FOUR

THE STATE

Our government exists to serve us, to serve the people. It does not exist to serve the stock market, nor to serve the international community.

The primary problem I see with the national government today is that it has become too complex. Its operations have become illegible to its own citizens, thus discouraging them from asserting responsibility for its actions. When citizens are unable to clearly assign responsibility, democratic sovereignty becomes attenuated and enfeebled, and the system's ability to benefit from appropriately directed discontent is destroyed.

However, the American conservative movement today has this harmful preoccupation with the size of government. While there are deep disagreements about the legitimate purposes of government, de-emphasizing important questions about the purpose of government has led conservatives to focus exclusively on questions about the government's size. Size is important, as many fiscal questions are a consequence of programs slated to grow unsustainably large—especially health-care entitlements. But the size of government is where the conversation ends.

One major obstacle is that both of our major political parties in the United States have developed approaches to knowledge and power that are not conducive to conservative thinking. Today, Democrats are deeply committed to a vision of scientifically backed technology; Republicans are so violently opposed to the idea of expertise that they seem at times to reject empiricism altogether.

It's like when all the right ever speaks of is a need to limit the terms of office, to cut the pay for that service, or make these the kinds of jobs that most of us would find miserable. What kind of people do you think will bother to run for office? You get what you pay for. And what do you suppose the motivation of the people who seek those offices might be then?

Could it be they're too incompetent to be making a decent wage in the private sector? Could it be they're seeking power? It could be that they are good hearted souls who are willing to put off making money for a few years because they want the best for our country. But I am not willing to gamble that's the primary motivating force for most people running for office, particularly if we don't provide an adequate salary to compensate someone.

The right, but also the left, is centered on arguing over the New Deal and Great Society still. It's a big fight over big government vs. limited government. It was a debate about how to reform America in an industrial mid-20th century world. But that debate is mostly resolved. But there is a new debate about the transformation to the post-industrial, Information Age, global economy.

But the right focuses too much on the question of big government versus small government, which itself discourages asking more important and fundamental questions: what should the government do and why? What is the purpose of a given program or regulation? How well, if at all, is it fulfilling that purpose? How do we know? If it is not fulfilling its purpose, what are the relevant alternatives? Focusing too much on size instead of purpose wastes time and attention that would be better used to make government more effective for the people we serve.

IMMIGRATION

America is the only country in the world whose immigration system puts the needs of other nations ahead of our own, and that must change. That's why I believe all immigration to the United States, legal or illegal, should be paused for a time.

All of the focus of the right on building the border wall or hordes of immigrants amassing on the Rio Grande misses the most significant source of illegal immigrants: overstayed visas. The Center for Migration Studies of New York found that in 2016-2017, people who overstayed their visas accounted for 62 percent of new illegal immigrants, while 38 percent had crossed a border illegally. They come with permission to enter our nation, to study, do business, or attend a conference, but they simply do not leave.

So, if you say you're a conservative politician who cares about ending illegal immigration but aren't willing to take on overstayed visas as well, then you're not serious about the issue.

And it doesn't make any sense to allow more people to enter America while we fix our system and decide what to do with the tens of millions of people who are here but have no right to be in this country in the first place. I sympathize with those people; they are in an extremely tough spot. But frankly, the United States is not the world's dumping ground for every third-world country and their refugees. We have no moral obligation to let in any immigrants or to let them stay.

Importantly, we have to acknowledge the source of the problem: immigrants aren't taking your jobs away; it's the fact that technology is pushing our economy in a direction that's making it harder and harder for Americans to get by on this "I trade my time for money" model.

The idea of not only drastically reducing illegal immigration but also a reduction even in legal immigration is a shocking thing to libertarians and conservatives who think of themselves as classical liberals. Chamber of Commerce Republicans argue that more immigration is always a good thing because it's always going to be economically beneficial because human beings are going to bring their productive capacities with them. Immigrants, even illegal immigrants, are going to pay into the Social Security system, and that all of this is really the thing that should be most important to us, and the aspirations of the immigrants, as opposed to the cultures from which they come.

The Republican Party wants to blame the Biden administration for a problem on the southern border that the party can solve. At the request of Texas Governor Greg Abbott, multiple Republican governors bragged about sending state troopers or national guard to the border. Of course, those deployments were for show and just a public relations stunt, but it also puts establishment Republicans in a bad place because it showed that the GOP isn't powerless—the GOP can exercise tremendous power if it wanted to. That's why the Republican elite wants to focus on Biden; they don't want to be pressured to go beyond publicity stunts and use the tools and power they have to secure the border.

Average Republican voters always want better trade deals and less immigration, while the Republican elites just want to give some platitude about not using big government to fix a problem. All the elites have been able to provide the voters with is, "we're going to cut your taxes; that's a priority; less immigration is never going to happen. But you still have to vote for us because we're good on abortion and we're good on gun control."

That is no longer enough for most people.

◆

Immigration is, fundamentally, an economic question. The Chamber of Commerce, Conservative Inc., and aligned think tanks like to pretend that there is a perpetual labor shortage that requires more immigration to alleviate that fake crisis. It's the very narrative being used as I write this chapter; the solution to the labor shortage America is experiencing is bringing in more immigrants to do the work. But how much cheap labor do we allow in our nation? Cheap labor that will drag down wages for workers in the agricultural, industrial, technology, and service sectors?

Of course, there are cultural elements to immigration; you'd have to be a liar to pretend those don't exist.

But Americans have every right to question our immigration policies' effect on our economy and society. In a serious country, citizens would be able to ask those questions without being labeled as xenophobes or racists.

Yet too often, the border crisis is framed as a humanitarian issue of the people coming here without any consideration for the Americans who are affected by this mass migration, many of whom are recent immigrants themselves. Why does the question never revolve around them?

A central argument for allowing more immigration made by the corporate Republicans and left-wing elite is one of boosting America's birth rate, which has been in marked decline for several years. Instead, they would import more people to serve them as a permanent underclass rather than allow for any policy that provides for increasing native population growth. If we want to encourage natural population growth, in addition to subsidizing old age, we also need to support that critical period of people's lives where they're financially strained, young in their earning lives, don't have enough wealth saved up to get on the property ladder, and don't feel confident enough to have children.

When our society is structured in a way that it's like a human shredder, we're going to find ourselves inviting more immigrants in. But the dirty little secret is that in one or two generations, the birth rates of the immigrants you brought in will converge with the native birth rate because of our society's socio-economic and social pressures. That's how powerful American assimilation is and why the elites will continue to call for more and more immigrants.

There are other societal costs to shipping more immigrants into America as well. In societies where the population is falling, natives' responses to immigration become more hostile because they feel like they're being replaced. Hostile not just to the immigrants but also to all others, including those of their own race or ethnicity. That situation does not end well for anybody.

My view is that the country is a vital part of our identity. The land, the place where our jurisdiction operates; it's a defense of territorial jurisdiction against religious or quasi-religious jurisdictions like the universal doctrine of human rights. We live in countries where the law is defined by the land over which it operates. And within that land, there is a sense of belonging, on which the law draws for the democratic process.

We're settled among neighbors. We want to get along with them. We don't want to force them to agree with us about everything. Nor do we require them to be of the same race, but we do require them to share our commitment to the place where we are. Because this is where we are building a home, other people might want to come into that home, and we should be entitled to invite them, provided they agree to abide by the rules. All this is perfectly reasonable.

It's all part of a democracy. We live in a place; we have the right to exclude from that place those we don't think will fit into it or to whom we don't want to extend a welcome. If we didn't have that right, we wouldn't feel secure occupying the place we claim as ours. It's a simple part of human nature.

GOVERNMENT SPENDING

In order to know what to fix with the government, we need to figure out what we want the government to do and go from there. Government budgets must be rewritten from scratch at all levels. Taxation needs to be simplified, lowered, and exemptions eliminated. That is the way we will be able to update our tax codes and not needlessly waste money.

Everyone in America knows that the government has spent far more for decades than it has raised in taxes. While politicians like to pretend we can someday balance our budget by simply cutting "waste, fraud, and abuse," we can't—and not because there isn't any waste or abuse in government. Roughly 45 percent of the national budget is just Social Security, Medicare, and Medicaid. About 15 percent is defense. And about 6 percent is the interest payment on the existing debt.

Just to stop borrowing, we would have to cut almost half or more of everything else the government does— the courts, FBI, FDA, EPA, CIA, and the rest—which is far more than any amount of inefficiency or waste we'll ever find. The problem is utterly unsolvable mathematically without reforms so dramatic that they will devastate people and the economy.

First off, the national budget, state budgets, local budgets, and so on need to be rewritten from the ground up. Forget about what's there now, the programs you want to keep, a specific number you might have in your mind; forget it all. Rewrite the budgets from scratch. We need to figure out what we want the government to do and go from there.

So, if I had unlimited power, I would start with the entitlement programs: Social Security, Medicaid, Medicare, and the hodgepodge of welfare programs we have. I would eliminate them all and set up a new streamlined system to provide direct assistance to our downtrodden citizens. This method has several benefits, beginning with getting rid of all the bureaucratic ossification that has accumulated since the 1930s.

I'd start with entitlements because those items made up 49 percent of the total federal budget in the 2020 fiscal year. You can complain about the million dollars here and million dollars there like so many of the dishonest politicians that yearly complain about it, but those savings are a statistical error in comparison.

For all the people preparing the pitchforks and torches for my daring to suggest we alter entitlements, why does the particular structure of how people receive payments matter so much to you? If people get the same or increased amounts of assistance, who really cares how it's done?

Likewise, with respect to the rest of the federal budget, I would go through every department and agency and figure out what needs to be done and who should be doing it. With 24,000 State Department employees, why is the United States still using a 19th-century model? How many are actually needed to perform diplomatic work in the 21st century?

These are the types of questions our leaders need to be asking. Just because things have always been done a certain way doesn't mean they need to be. Of course, there are times when changes are not required, but we need more than "just because." What to do with all these newly unneeded civil servants? I would debrief them all, buy out their pensions and retirements with tax-free lump-sum payments, and wish them all happy lives outside of government. There's no reason to be mean about eliminating career bureaucrats.

Then comes the question of taxes. Continuing in this scenario, I would lower tax rates, combine the individual tax brackets from seven to four, and eliminate all the ways people are currently able to deduct from taxes. Get rid of the capital gains tax; now that would be taxed under the individual income tax.

Get rid of the stepped-up basis, and if you don't know what that is, here's a little explainer: What a lot of billionaires do is, rather than taking a larger salary or selling an asset they own, they will borrow against it for the course of their lifetime. That way, they're not realizing a gain and not even having to pay capital gains taxes on it. When they die and leave the assets to their heirs, that is when the stepped-up basis comes into play. Their heirs are able to recognize that asset at the new level without having to pay taxes on any of the increase in value.

These are just the initial steps I would take so we could stabilize our situation and give America breathing room to figure out what to do next.

THE ORIGINAL AMERICAN SYSTEM

True conservative economics is not the neoliberal economic ideal of tax cuts and deregulation; instead, it is the ambitious nationalist economic policy agendas of Alexander Hamilton and Henry Clay, the American System. Yet the American right has outsourced our economic thinking to neoliberals such as Milton Friedman and Friedrich Hayak, who had very compelling arguments in the 1960s and 1970s, but those ideas do not account for the situation of today's world and today's economy.

The American System represents the legacy of Alexander Hamilton, America's first Secretary of the Treasury. In his *Report on Manufactures*, Hamilton argued that the United States would never be truly independent until it was self-sufficient when it came to vital economic products and was not economically or financially dependent on Britain or other European powers. That the creation of a strong central government that was able to promote science, invention, industry, and commerce was essential to promoting the general welfare and making the economy of the United States strong enough to allow the nation to determine its own destiny.

In Hamilton's *Report on Manufactures*, he proposed subsidies and protection in the form of tariffs for the nascent manufacturing industry in America. Hamilton argued that manufacturing would allow for a far more efficient division of labor, and a better matching of talents and capacities to occupations would encourage immigration to extend each of these benefits further. He saw it would be immensely useful to the new nation and concluded that it was only sensible for the government to encourage it actively.

Opponents to Hamilton's plan, primarily plantation owners in the southern states, emphasized the problems with subsidizing specific sectors and businesses, in particular the potential for corruption and sectional favoritism. As such, the tariffs were implemented, but not the subsidies. As political constituencies grew up around them, the tariffs quickly became much higher than what Hamilton had proposed.

Despite the partial implementation of his suggestions, Hamilton's basic insight that the enormous economic value that innovative industries could offer the nation merited public efforts to enable their success has always had strong adherents in national politics. In the decades leading up to the Civil War, the federal government intervened strategically in markets to spur innovation, frequently exercised its constitutionally enumerated power to grant patents, and even encouraged and protected Americans who stole industrial secrets from Great Britain—at the time, the world leader in manufacturing technology.

After Hamilton, Henry Clay took up the cause following the War of 1812 with a government-sponsored program to harmonize and balance the nation's agriculture, commerce, and industry. He created the American System, which consisted of three parts: tariffs to protect and promote American industry; a national bank; and federal subsidies for roads, canals, trains, and other internal improvements, with the funds for the subsidies being paid for from the tariffs and sale of public lands. His plan's goal was to transform the United States from a group of sectionally divided agricultural states tightly linked to British manufacturing into a unified, dynamic industrial economy.

Abraham Lincoln accelerated this process dramatically by expanding the infrastructure of railways and telegraphs, increasing tariffs, establishing a system of national banks and the Department of Agriculture, and land-grant colleges that ultimately created agricultural experiment stations to promote innovation on farms.

The American System continued to be championed by Republicans well into the early 20th century. President Calvin Coolidge remarked, "Our only defense against the cheap production, low wages and low standard of living which exist abroad, and our only method of maintaining our own standards, is through a protective tariff. We need protection as a national policy, to be applied wherever it is required."

It is this tradition on which the right can build a new system.

A NEW AMERICAN SYSTEM

The free-market fundamentalism that afflicts our nation now results from conservatives' losing sight of who was supposed to lead whom. The American system was set up by prudent statesmen using public policy to direct business toward socially beneficial ends. In practice, leaders have often been content to be led instead of leading. Politicians owe their responsibility not to big business and the chamber of commerce but to the individual citizens they represent, and their policies have got to be what's best for the people. Big business interests are profits over people, and they are willing to sell this country down the river.

What party today can credibly claim to be restoring the American dream for the middle class? The middle class is decomposing in this country; some people are filtering up into a higher echelon, but most people are filtering down and becoming more precarious, and you'll find that millennials aren't able to form families like our Gen-X counterparts or Boomers before them.

The American dream is dying. We're not having as many children as we want to have, not buying homes, not attaining the level of wealth other generations have at our age, and it's getting worse for the Zoomers below us. This American dream that if I get an education and if I basically work hard and play by the rules at whatever I choose to do, I have a fair shot of attaining the living standards my parents had or even maybe improving on them. I don't think Republicans have wrapped their minds around this yet.

The right feels the need to have market solutions to every social problem. I favor market solutions where they apply, but not every social problem requires a market solution. There is a need to maintain traditions in education, culture, and the law, which are not traditions of free enterprise but much more traditions of collective renunciation of one's own individuality.

The debate between "socialism" and reckless, endless, unsustainable neoliberal consumerism is a false dichotomy. We can create a healthy, sustainable, nationalist market economy that works for American families. Free markets are simply a tool to allocate resources and structure economies effectively. They do not need to be protected absolutely. Free trade may benefit the conservative donor class, but it doesn't benefit the ordinary conservative voter.

Once again, the goals of the right should not be to achieve tax cuts or deregulation. They should be to rebuild American families, restore American sovereignty, and revitalize American culture. The system I want to return to is one based on a free-market economy overlaid with specific interventions to provide infrastructure and to promote incremental, innovation-led growth. The economic vision of Hamilton, Clay, and Lincoln can pave the way for America to rebuild our industry and our nation.

Trade protection and an ambitious economic policy are the keys to rebuilding America. Our priority has to be building a healthy society, not the free-market.

MOVING FORWARD

For years now, I have heard countless Republican politicians use the same old neoliberal lines about cutting taxes, the importance of immigration, worrying about business interests, and most importantly, not using government power. In other words, to keep the political status quo. Yet, they failed to realize that our economy exists to serve us, to serve people. Not to serve the Chamber of Commerce, not to serve multinational corporations.

I also believe in the free market. I reject and abhor socialism. I think it's a terrible way to organize your economy. But in cases when the most efficient outcome for the market, which is what it always tries to achieve, is not good for America, then I think we should do something about it.

It may be more efficient to make protective equipment for a pandemic or pharmaceuticals in China, but I'm not sure most people agree that's in our national interest. It may be the most efficient outcome for all kinds of industrial capacity to relocate overseas, but it's not in our national interest to have entire communities gutted, thousands upon thousands of good-paying, stable jobs wiped out. And the nation loses industrial capacity. And it's those instances where I want government to, when it has to choose between the efficient and the national interest, to choose the national interest.

I think that one of the biggest policy shortcomings of the conservative movement for the last however many years is on health care. We have got to have an answer to the Medicare For All debate. But right now, all we have is a partial answer that nobody is satisfied with, and the public is rightly upset about that. Every different international system is completely different, and they have different rules, different regulations, et cetera, but they all push towards a system where a family feels financially secure in their health care decisions.

We don't have that, and we need to have it as a party. I think if we're going to build a stable coalition over many years, it needs to be something that we own because it's so central to what should be the governing principle of conservatism, in my opinion, which is to create a system where stable and secure families have a place to grow and prosper. And without that health care piece, I think we're going to be fighting an uphill battle.

The notion that we have a truly libertarian free-market is a myth. Anytime you apply rules on an economy, the economy is going to behave accordingly. So, we have rules now, but, in many cases, they incentivize the wrong things. They incentivize taking the money your company made, and rather than reinvesting it to grow and create new jobs, the incentive is to buy back shares to increase the value on the stock market to make shareholders happy. There's nothing illegal about that, nor should there be, but why do we incentivize that?

What we should be incentivizing is that if you just buy back shares, the taxing authorities will treat that as if it was a dividend. But if instead you take that money and invest it in building new facilities and new jobs, that's where the incentive and benefit will come from.

END OF THE NEW DEAL AGE

America as a whole is going to continue to solve social problems, but we're not going to do it in a New Deal framework, where when you have a problem, you create a new program and a new agency, you give it to a bunch of experts and they will administer and plan progress. We're not doing that again anymore. So, we need to solve problems in a different way.

We need to throw away the archaic messages of New Deal liberalism or fighting big government and instead construct a completely different message from scratch. A new ideology that can create a new agenda that actually speaks to the problems that keep Americans up at night. This message would recognize the fears most Americans share about their future. It would explain what exactly is broken in America and propose what must be done to fix it. And provide a framework to build a positive agenda of ideas to make the future better.

On the right, you have economic fundamentalists telling these economically distressed areas to just wait for the invisible hand of the market to rescue them, and on the left, there are these cultural liberals who subscribe to an increasingly militant form of identity politics. What both do lead to this social atomization and fragmentation. What we need is a politics that can talk about the common good and the things like institutions, traditions, and common stories that bring us together and help us remember that we have these inclusive identities.

I'd love to be able to say there's a secret formula for advancing the right, but the truth is it's simple. Elect a new generation to office. The same officials who got us into this mess aren't going to get us out. But in order to do that, the current officeholders need to recognize they need to move on and not cling to power.

But even Millennial leaders like Representatives Elise Stefanik and Dan Crenshaw have made huge names for themselves but have just put a new face on the old neoliberal ideology. At the same time, in other parts of the country, Republicans are just retreading the same old tired faces, faces that lose us seats. Continuing to the run the same people for the same offices or running a game of musical chairs will lead the Republican Party to waking up one day soon to being swept from office in historically reliably conservative states like Texas, South Carolina, or even Nebraska.

All of our assumptions, whether it's politics or the economy, are built around a group of assumptions that life in America looks like it did in the mid-20th century. That's no longer true. That's why we're having all these problems. It's why our tax system is falling apart.

The only answers we have right now are either new agencies and new programs or fighting big government, and it's a non-sequitur to this whole new set of problems. If we want to compete and not go into a decline, we have to take all our institutions, the way we work, our tax system, how we regulate everything, and take all of them and build in these new assumptions of how we work and live in an Information Age economy. That means reforming everything.

There are big problems people need to solve, but all the parties can talk about is fighting over the New Deal. It's all just rhetoric now. I think we all know there's not going to be another Great Society and that we aren't abolishing Social Security and Medicare. The institutions we created in the New Deal that are still here are permanent for the most part, unless they get reformed in some other way. Republicans can campaign on social security privatization all they want, but it's not going to happen and we all know it.

We cannot continue electing these technically incompetent people who grew up in an era before the Great Society programs, born in the 1950s or even 1940s, and who are not capable of living in a 21st-century technological world with all this change. We are in a new age, so we need leaders who understand how things work.

CHAPTER FIVE

FOREIGN POLICY

American foreign policy is one area where the left and right elites unite, in this case, under the banner of war-mongering for the express purpose of giving the military-industrial complex more money.

The elites have no problem throwing the entire weight of the United States government behind their pet projects abroad, which usually means overthrowing foreign governments to install dictators that have a favorable, at first, view of the United States. This is the reality of the world we live in. But it's based on the fantasy that the liberal world order is the best thing for the world, or even for western nations.

America's foreign policy should reject internationalism and move towards transactional realism. It is in America's interest to focus more on what's happening here at home than it is to frolic through foreign nations, blow up the governments we don't like, then attempt (and fail) to establish a Western-style democracy. Our current philosophy of intervening in or staying in other nations for humanitarian reasons is entirely reliant on the idea that only American views matter. Who cares about other people's traditions or their own laws when America knows best? The thing is, we don't.

Despite what the war hawks say, restraint is not pacifism. The United States has limited responsibility to others as it conducts its foreign policy. This view is not naive about how the world works; it understands that the United States and other countries have interests, have strategic challenges and threats, and need a strong national defense to defend against the possibilities of other actors aggressing against us. The primary responsibility nations have is to their own, so the argument that America has weighty moral responsibilities to settle foreign civil conflicts isn't supported by simple reason.

Our foreign policy should solely revolve around the defense of our nation, not some delusional neoliberal vision of a global American order. That means realism and restraint; realism about the world around us and restraint in using our military power only to advance American national interests. We should have a strong national defense, second to none, but we don't need to go abroad to find monsters to destroy or remaking other societies by the point of a sword. We don't need to do that. Doing that gets us into trouble and undermines our nation in the eyes of the world.

Having a large, permanent, professional army is too big a temptation for our generals and leaders to use for whatever purpose they want. We know this because they keep using it in far-away places on flimsy explanations that are somehow in America's national interest. If we have an army, we should keep it inside our borders to protect us. I'm reasonably sure that Germany and Japan are not eagerly anticipating the day American troops leave those countries to restart their plans for world conquest and domination.

If we ever needed to build the army back up to full war footing, we still have a navy and air force that can respond quickly to any situation in the world and defend America while an army is being assembled. Our satellites and spy planes can monitor the entire surface of our planet, so any surprise attack on the American homeland or against our allies with large numbers of infantry and land-based vehicles will be seen. Relying on a strong navy and air force, which cannot occupy land, is sufficient protection while also preventing war hawks from just invading a small country for the hell of it.

There are also extraordinarily relevant questions for developing future American foreign policy, partic-ularly in light of the last 20 to 30 years of disaster that

America has experienced. Experience has shown that you can't just copy and paste the Constitution into Iraq and Afghanistan or wherever else and create a bunch of mini-Americas. If neoconservatives really believed in American exceptionalism, they would realize that the American people are exceptional and unique.

Most importantly, when it comes to foreign policy matters, America needs to be pragmatic. Ideals have their place, but it is not a viable strategy when facing other nations who may not share the same values or want to harm us. Looking back on the last 100 years of American foreign policy leaves me with many questions, starting with who are we to educate the rest of the world on democracy and freedom? Who are we to tell other nations how to structure their societies when we can barely run our own?

Despite its portrayal in pop culture, the American military has limitations and the top brass is totally incompetent. It's a consequence of the military brass having a culture not based on merit but on towing the party line. The focus of Joint Chiefs of Staff Chairman Mark Milley on making shows of diversity for diversity's sake (not on military readiness) shows that the military is not immune from the rot that infects the rest of our institutions.

Meanwhile, our national security class is dysfunctional and puts other countries' interests before America's, especially at the U.S. border. But I think bringing our armies home from across the world and putting

200,000 troops on the U.S. border would be the most popular foreign policy move in the last 200 years.

AFGHANISTAN

I know it's fashionable to blame the Biden regime for the mess in Afghanistan and say that the Trump administration wouldn't have cocked things up. It's true; the Biden administration was totally incompetent here and made a total mess. But the only reason Trump wouldn't have done this poorly is that the generals would have convinced Trump to stay in Afghanistan and go back on his word and the peace deal he made with the Taliban. America would not have left in that case.

When it comes to the Afghanistan withdrawal, people fall into one of two camps: Either you wanted to get out of Afghanistan, accepting that it wasn't going to be sunshine and rainbows leaving a failed 20-year project, or you wanted to stay and have the blood of more soldiers on your hands. Those are the only choices.

Which makes me want to make the supporters of staying in Afghanistan say it's okay for 22-year olds to be blown to bits by a suicide bomb for a corrupt government and an endless mission. Why don't they have to defend 20 years of a failed war, thousands of American dead, tens of thousands of wounded, and the countless Afghans who have been killed in this war? How much money did we waste over there? Why don't they go ahead and defend that instead of trying to make saving American's lives is some terrible thing?

We spent $6.4 trillion in Iraq and Afghanistan. We could have rebuilt our crumbling highways. Reinforced and hardened the electrical grid. You can completely replace the entire United States naval fleet with the most advanced generations of ships and still have tens, hundreds of billions of dollars to spare.

That is the hypocrisy of neoliberals on the left and right; they won't blink an eye at spending ungodly amounts of money on illegal wars that have long ended, but when there's a chance to make the average American's lives better, even just a little bit, that's when they're all concerned about the national debt and deficits. The doublespeak is disgusting.

The devastation from our pullout of Afghanistan does pull at people's heartstrings, and it's horrifically sad. But what exactly are the opponents of withdrawal really arguing for? Do you think just keeping the few thousand troops we had there would do anything for women's rights or would do anything for pushing back the Taliban? No, and they know it.

At this point, Afghanistan's future is in the hands of its people. It may sound highly callous, but what is the alternative? Sending in hundreds of thousands of American troops? If you're going to say anything about the Taliban's trampling of women's rights or human rights, then what about MBS and the Saudis and their horrific treatment of people? Are they next on the invasion list? Of course not.

So, let's not pretend that any of the hand wringing is about women's rights or human rights or anything of the sort. It's about money and power for the people who get rich off of these kinds of conflicts. The American people have been lied to by both parties about the situation on the ground in Afghanistan. There was nothing left to be gained by staying in Afghanistan. It was a puppet government propped up by the American military that folded under the slightest breeze.

Don't be fooled by the neocons trying to grift off this conversation simply because they are anti-Biden. If people like Lindsey Graham or Ben Sasse had their way, we'd be in Afghanistan for another 20 years, and they have been pretty open about this. Al Qaeda doesn't need Afghanistan to do what it's trying to do, and we don't need a permanent military presence in Afghanistan to fight them.

We could not do anything well in Afghanistan. Obama surged the troops, and the violence got worse. As Trump increased the bombing campaign and casualties, the Taliban kept gaining. Instead of massive incompetence being a reason to leave, it's an excuse to stay. "Give us just a few months." Yeah, right.

We gave the Afghan National Security forces $100 billion to rebuild and equip themselves. We gave them every chance we could to fight for their own country, and they folded within three weeks. They were so corrupt and inept that they fell like a house of cards.

And it was way worse than we thought. We were lied to even more than we thought. Presidents were lied to routinely, and our military lied to themselves. The bottom line is the Afghan military was fake, the Afghan government was fake, the development aid was fake; all we did was create a system of kleptocracy that had zero local support. Our money was wasted and squandered, and lives were lost for literally nothing.

This was the outcome in Afghanistan no matter how long we stayed. So, who's to blame?

The intelligence community kept us there under false pretenses. The Pentagon had 18 months to plan for the withdrawal. The same for the State Department. Why did it take so long to process special Afghan visas? They didn't think the United States would actually pull out. They dragged their feet on all of this. What would the neoliberals have us do? Stay on for another five years? I blame them all.

Like it or not, we had a peace agreement with the Taliban. If we hadn't started pulling American troops out by May 1, 2021, then they would have started attacking American troops again. This loss is not on our soldiers who lost their lives or limbs there. It is on the generals, and it is on the politicians and leaders who sent them there.

In the end, the quickness of the end of the Afghan government lends credence to the idea that the government didn't have the legitimacy, the staying power, or the ability to govern without the coalition backing it up, and suggests America's 20-year project of nation-building was an utter failure and lends support to our withdrawal.

ALLIANCES

World War II ended 76 years ago, and the Cold War ended 32 years ago. So why does the United States still have over 100,000 soldiers stationed throughout Europe? I know that the stated purpose is to disincentivize the Soviets, now Russia, from invading western Europe, but I'm not sure Russia would even want to march on Paris or Rome, if they even had the capability.

Of course, the war hawks on the left and right still stupidly imagine Russia as America's greatest adversary. They are fixated on Russian President Vladimir Putin as evil incarnate, and while I have no love for Putin, I do not despise him either. He is doing what he thinks is best for Russia, but those actions confound so many in the American national security apparatus because he wants to advance Russian interests, not American. That is a massive flaw in thinking for America.

It is concerning that Russia and China have been growing closer together. However, eventually, the Chinese will get greedy and attempt, by trick or by military might, to take from Russia all its eastern territories, which have vast amounts of natural resources that have been mainly untapped. Once Russia figures out what the Chinese are up to, northern Asia will be the most significant flashpoint, greater than anything else in the world right now.

As I write this, the situation in the Russo-Ukrainian War of 2022 continues to be very fluid and up in the air. Yes, the war hawks are terrible people and have this deep-seated desire for regime change and to get the United States into action as an active participant. But that doesn't make everything skeptics of foreign intervention say correct either. I have seen plenty of war skeptics tweeting just god-awful takes, thinking they are dunking on the war hawks and feeling so smug about it.

The skeptics make up for their lack of knowledge of geopolitics and foreign affairs by substituting in domestic American political and cultural war dynamics. Worst of all, a number of loud voices in that space are entirely defeatist. They are saying that Ukraine should just roll over, demilitarize themselves, and let Russia take control. Who the hell thinks like that?

Ukraine and every other nation have the ability to align themselves with whoever they want, and their neighbors don't get to decide for them. If America was invaded, would the skeptics be saying just let it happen? No, of course not!

This leads me to a primary tool America uses to extend its imperial power: the North Atlantic Treaty Organization, or NATO.

It was useful when the Soviets were threatening central and western Europe, but its purpose of containing Russia ended with the fall of the Soviet Union. And the question needs to be asked: against whom are we protecting ourselves against with the NATO alliance?

The reasoning of President Trump, brought up early in his administration, that many member nations do not meet the treaty spending requirements on defense is certainly an excellent place to start. If our allies aren't willing to make that investment in their own national security, why should American taxpayers subsidize that? I have my own concerns, starting with how American forces have been tied up in Europe for the last 75 years when they could be here at home or positioned closer to where future conflicts are expected in southwest Asia or the South China Sea.

Now, I will not deny that there are compelling reasons to keep American membership in NATO, but I cannot and will not accept the war hawk's talking points that the greatest threat to America from now to the end of time is Russia. Nor do I think that withdrawing from NATO means that America should hide itself in the western hemisphere or that America should even withdraw from NATO.

When the fallout from the Russo-Ukrainian War of 2022 settles down, America and European countries need to make an open and sincere offer to Russia to join our clubs and revitalize their European side, like what happened with East Germany and Eastern Europe.

The point of this is to ally ourselves with Russia against China, with whom Russia has a very superficial relationship.

Afterwards, the United States should take a back seat in NATO. Still be involved, but let Europe take the lead with it.

Instead, the future of American foreign policy should be built on the foundation of the Anglosphere—the United States, United Kingdom, Canada, Australia, and New Zealand—nations that share a common language, common history, and traditions rooted in common law and basic liberty. Not only that, we currently share intelligence with those other nations under the Five Eyes agreement, and under the AUKUS pact for submarines and now hypersonic missiles.

They are our natural friends and allies due to the fact that, for a not insignificant number of Americans, they are our cousins. In a turbulent world like this, that should be the leading alliance America identifies with. This doesn't even include other nations based on UK common law, such as Ireland, India, South Africa, and the English-speaking Caribbean, which America would find ideologically similar countries to ally with in times of trouble.

CHINA

America is fortunate to be surrounded by major oceans and have some degree of geographic distance from the rest of the world, but we have often assumed that we have a singular point of agency in deciding how our foreign policy is run. But the reality is that the world is dynamic and interactive, and our foreign policy really needs to be based on the foreign policy of the other major players in the world that we're engaging with. It takes two to tango.

We can have the best intentions and want peace, but ultimately, if you're interacting with a country that is engaging in a grey war with you, you're not going to be met at the altar. And you're going to see things like the massive deindustrialization of your country and a lot of other adverse side effects take place that are ultimately not going to be in your interests.

America need to remain militarily strong and develop advanced technologies to beat back future adversaries such as China.

With most conflicts globally, the United States doesn't need to be involved; we don't need to have boots on the ground or even over the horizon capabilities. A conflict with a rising power like China is different because they aren't some third-rate dictatorship whose air force can be destroyed with a cruise missile or two; they do have the potential to hurt the American homeland economically and militarily.

This makes things insane when you consider that in 2020, net imports from China rose 54% because the Trump administration talked Donald Trump out of signing a Buy American executive order that was ready and sitting in the National Security Council because his advisors didn't want to piss off the Chinese and to ensure that we could continue to have just-in-time delivery. We are all getting taxed, effectively, for the failure of administration after administration to make the American economy more resilient.

At the tactical level, we need to deglobalize China's technology infrastructure that lets it have intrusive access to other countries' data ranging from computer networks to telecommunications, by making it attractive for those other nations to buy American technology instead. This can partly be done by resolving the conflict between parts of our business community and our national security priorities.

A fundamental purpose for any government is to provide for the common defense. As such, a core function of our government should be to say what's okay and not okay when it comes to doing business with a foreign adversary like China. There needs to be a framework that articulates that the American government has the authority to review any investments by American firms in China on national security grounds, similar to the investments made by Chinese firms and nationals that are reviewed on national security grounds.

Our past policies of engagement and having a very collaborative approach have not worked out the way we thought. It led to a massive military buildup on the Chinese side. The erosion of American deterrence in the East Asia Pacific has served us a great disservice. The AUKUS deal is an excellent step towards restoring that deterrence.

China's navy recently built 350 ships, and this is the key to their path of invading Taiwan. If we want to deter them, we have to have an asymmetric capacity to sink their navy. We have to be honest about that. That doesn't mean we'll do it, but just having the capacity will deter them from trying, and giving more subs to allied nations like Australia, Japan, or South Korea lessens the likelihood of a Chinese invasion that much more.

The biggest signal America can make is abandoning the strategy of ambiguity, meaning we may or may not intervene militarily if Taiwan is attacked. By showing we may intervene, it keeps China in check and makes them have second thoughts.

Taiwan's Defense Minister said he believes China could conduct a full land invasion by 2025. How do we stop that? Use the old adage of speaking softly and carrying a big stick. In this case, the big stick would be stationing American troops in Taiwan to really make the Chinese think before attacking. Because who really thinks China wants an all-out war with the United States?

Beyond China's immediate vicinity to Taiwan, how do their actions threaten our system and our way of life? It's because of computer chips, maritime routes, and precedent. We're not going to have computer chips if China takes Taiwan, or their integrity will be severely compromised with backdoors built into them, so China has direct access to our communications and systems. We won't be able to guarantee access or the integrity of the chips if China seizes Taiwan.

Vietnam isn't the best analogy for domino theory, but the interwar period is, with Germany invading Czechoslovakia and the Sudetenland. As the Taiwan Strait is a major maritime corridor of global trade, a Chinese invasion would give them a significant amount of leverage over controlling that corridor which is another choke point that could have enormous repercussions on our economy. When you have an ambitious, autocratic, revisionist power that is fueled by a feeling of resentment, you need to draw a really clear line in the sand; otherwise, they'll go after more. Mongolia, other islands, and you need to draw a line in the sand somewhere, or you're going to find yourself on your back foot and in a weakened position to respond.

If you want to do the right thing for the security of America, you basically have two options. Force a hard divestment, an actual divestment, which means it's not just a divestment of the corporate entity like Microsoft buying Tik Tok; you actually have to divest the company from China's jurisdictional reach. Move the servers, move the engineers, all of the infrastructure out of China so that China can't get to it. Or you ban them in the U.S.

When you extrapolate a few years from now and be honest that we are not friends with China, the fact that Taiwan sees a full-scale invasion as possible by 2025 means the future of US-China diplomatic relations is very uncertain. That raises a lot of big questions; in a world where our diplomatic relations are in question, what does that mean for our supply chains there? What does that mean for Apple? What does that mean for all the companies that rely on steady, stable diplomatic relations?

It is vitally essential for the macro-economic stability of our companies and our country to actually go through the very laborious legwork of figuring out what the bucket of goods that are not critical to national security is. We don't care where it comes from; the bucket of goods that are absolutely so vital that we need them to be made here in the U.S.; and the bucket of goods that are critical but could be made in some allied country that we trust. We need to figure that out pretty quickly because time is flying by us and doesn't give us much time to prepare for a really turbulent time in US-China relations.

CONCLUSION

We lost Iraq, we lost Afghanistan. We spent $6 trillion in nation building in just those two countries, and what do we have to show for that?

A lot of people who claim to be America First are actually just reactive, emotional people willing to be played by the media and neoconservatives because they hate Biden so much that it short-circuits their brains, making them forget what an actual foreign policy or what they claim to want looks like. We need to stop being a crusader state, imposing our vision over the face of the Earth.

No, the United States shouldn't have our forces physically intervene on the ground or in the air (in the form of a no-fly zone) in the current Ukraine conflict, but that doesn't mean sending weapons, ammunition, and cash to the Ukrainian government is a capitulation to the Biden agenda. There is so much more nuance to great power dynamics, and America can support our friends and allies to beat back invaders while keeping American troops out of the conflict while on alert in case things go sideways.

Honestly, I hate the snarky skeptics far more than the war hawks because, at least with the hawks, you know they just want the troops to fight. With the skeptics, particularly the ones who claim to be populists or nationalists, it is much harder to figure them out and what endgame they are aiming for. They're tone deaf and are so distrustful of everything, nihilistic, and just plain Debbie Downers, it's actually pretty sad. Sometimes, you do things because it's just the right thing to do as a human being. We can't let ourselves be heartless, uncaring bastards.

I understand that the war-mongers in both parties have this deep-seated desire to ruthlessly enforce western-style democracy on nearly every country on our planet, even those nations that have no such traditions or experience of it. It's the same philosophy of Jonah "Iraq was a worthy mistake" Goldberg and Stephen Hayes, who literally wrote a book on the (false) connection between Saddam Hussain and Osama Bin-Laden in the lead-up to the 2003 invasion of Iraq.

There's a recurring tendency in history for really smart people to assume we left behind the bad old days and are moving into a newer, more peaceful, more cooperative era. We've seen this in the late 1700s, at times in the 1800s, and at the beginning of the 1900s, and without exception, what happens is an individual or group of individuals come along and remind us that the world is as it always has been. Napoleon and the French Revolution played that role by taking Europe into a generation of war, we saw it in the 20th century with the fascist and communist leaders who really helped provoke conflicts of unprecedented death and savagery, and we're seeing it again today with Putin.

Maybe, just maybe, American democracy isn't the best system of government for every country out there.

Maybe America should let the people in other countries run their own countries and not have America endlessly meddle, which, nine times out of ten, makes things exponentially worse anyway.

Does America really want to keep the role of global hegemon, putting out every local brushfire while extending our imperial power over the entire planet?

I don't, not like this.

CHAPTER SIX

THE ECONOMY

Once upon a time, we Americans lived in an industrial-age economy in which a high school-educated worker could support a family in a middle-class lifestyle with a skilled manufacturing job. That worker's paycheck could buy a house in the suburbs, a car or two, a television and other modern appliances while his non-working spouse stayed home to raise the family full-time. That is no longer the case. Two-income households now are struggling to make ends meet and are living paycheck to paycheck, putting off having children or buying a home because they cannot afford either.

Yet, we continue to act and think of our work life in terms of the industrial-era labor relationship. We think of family life in terms of the traditional nuclear family unit, with one wage earner and one domestic worker in charge of child care. We think of foreign policy as if America was naturally a colossus, fighting for freedom and producing the world's materials. We believe it's natural that the world watches American movies, buys American cars, and uses American dollars as their reserve currency. We think it is our right that our middle-class ought to be wealthier than the middle-classes or even the upper-classes of most other nations.

Over decades, we built our informal and government institutions assuming these things were true because, for most of our lifetimes, they were. These assumptions quietly stood behind the Medicare system. They stood behind the Social Security system. They're the assumptions of the education system, America's environmental, labor, and health and safety laws, and the assumptions supporting the commitments of the federal budget. In short, they are the assumptions behind everything.

Not only are our institutions grounded in the assumptions of a mid-20th century industrial America, but our very politics are as well. This lost world continues to frame the thinking of both the left and the right, who often don't even realize they're presuming the long-gone world of the mid-20th century is America's natural order.

During that time, the primary debate was how best to manage and distribute the staggering fortune and wealth America's industrial economy was then producing. We fought over the most practical way to do it—whether the economic system was more efficiently managed by a group of carefully selected experts or by markets and bottom-up choices. We disputed the fairest way to do it; whether the fruits of America's labor should be distributed to citizens based primarily to those who produced them, or otherwise; and if so, how that could be fairly accomplished. We disputed the ideological underpinnings—how our cultural assumptions impacted the system and how the change would affect us.

Using that industrial-era model of the world in our heads, we built institutions to do these things—from Social Security to Medicare, the EPA, our tax code, family medical leaves, and so on—dividing our political system into two camps, each taking a different side. All of our institutions are built around that version of America and rely on the assumption that the mid-20th century industrial America is still a reality.

But that is no longer true.

OFF THE TRACKS

America's economy, culture, and position in the world are increasingly different from the industrial-era models that exist in our heads as "normal" because industrial-era America is almost gone and has been transformed into information-age America. This new economy is a fast, digital service economy with global competition coming from places Americans recently called the third-world.

One high-school educated adult can no longer expect to support a middle-class lifestyle with a factory job. Americans can no longer expect to work at one great American industrial firm for forty years and at retirement receive a pension, a gold watch, and the company's thanks. The new model of American life is not safe, stable, or effortlessly prosperous. It's fast, mobile, disruptive, and unstable.

Workers rapidly get laid off and change jobs; new technologies emerge every few years, disrupting new economic sectors. Cultural norms change constantly. Manufacturing and industrial-era jobs are replaced with service and information jobs. Americans compete against former subsistence farmers equipped with laptop computers and mobile phones from halfway around the globe.

Competition comes from everywhere—not only from China, India, Brazil, Russia, and Europe, but also from places many Americans don't think that much about, like Indonesia, Vietnam, Bangladesh, and more. American culture is increasingly competing with other cultures. People migrate across continents for opportunity and safety. Former Cold War allies no longer feel threatened enough to follow America's lead unquestioningly, and they look to rising powers everywhere who are seeking to take America's place. Although we're not sure what it means for the future, it's clear the industrial-era economy is gone. America will always manufacture things, but the world is no longer organized around our mass-produced industrial goods.

It is the altar of globalization and the altar of cheap prices—the great promise of neoliberalism and libertarianism—that have made us make terrible political choices over the last fifty years, making us less safe and less robust. There is a real benefit to being able to make things in America; to live in a town; to work in a factory that is producing something; and to have pride in your work and get paid a good wage. But after seeing the American government allow China into the World Trade Organization and establish permanent normal trade relations with China, and watching that factory go away at the snap of your fingers, it's easy to know why it went away.

Our political elite made that choice because they said, "Fuck you, you're better off; you have a cheaper TV now." They said the GDP would go up, which was great for some people but not for the average person. It is a deep rot in our society where the promise has been that if you have cheaper stuff and can buy more cheap Chinese crap, you're going to be happy. Everything has been done to justify those ends, and it hasn't made us happy, it hasn't made us satisfied, and it hasn't brought us any spiritual nourishment or together as a community.

A harsh consequence of the devotion towards this neoliberal thought is the collapse of unions in America and the nth-degree negative effects on the rights of all workers in our nation. Most workers' unions are run by left-wing activists who do not represent average workers at all, which is a big reason they have been unpopular in recent years. But what if the unions' enormous political power could help the right instead of the left? A competent right-wing movement could easily sway worker's unions from the left if it wanted to; in fact, that should be the right's goal.

Workers should have the means to come together to support each other, exert more power vis-à-vis capital in the labor market, and have more of a voice in the workplace. They are more allies to the right than the woke elites running the corporations today. We should want workers to have power in the labor market and be able to find themselves in collaboration with each other, which has substantive benefits towards what the right cares about: community.

If you want an economy that's generating widespread prosperity—spoiler warning, the market doesn't automatically just do that. We've seen that the market doesn't do that in recent decades. So, we have two choices: either we have an economy where workers have a relatively high level of power vis-à-vis employers to ensure that the prosperity generated in our economy reaches them, or we can use the government to redistribute wealth.

It should be evident to everyone which choice the right should support.

How much employees earn or what benefits they have through their employment are not the only concerns the right should have when it comes to workers. It would be ideal for parents to spend less time at their workplace and more time with their children as pro-family conservatives. We should want people to spend more time with their children.

Yet sometimes in our society, we fetishize working three jobs or walking 12 miles to get to your workplace, but that's not actually healthy. We live in a radically different society than in 1996. Fertility rates are falling, and child poverty is skyrocketing. The traditional "pull yourself up by your bootstraps" mentality hasn't worked since well before the great recession in 2008-2009.

The hardest hit in this respect are the Millennials, many of whom aren't able to form families like Gen-X or the Baby Boomers. We aren't buying homes, we aren't attaining the level of wealth previous generations had at our age, and most concerning is that we aren't having as many kids as we want to have. The middle class is dying with us; some are filtering up, but most are moving down, and their lives are becoming more precarious. We shouldn't have to uproot ourselves and our families in order to live a decent, middle-class life. Or make it that if we refuse to move, we will die or get hooked on opioids or meth.

Millennials see the hypocritical nature of the world while we are forced to choose between a soul-crushing corporate job or living in our hometowns with little to no prospects of having a decent career and being able to afford to raise a family. This is the choice millions of Millennials like me have been forced to make.

In this, compassion is needed; not lecturing people, saying that your life is better now that your job left here, or that since your job left here, it's now on you to move to another city. Many people enjoy where they're from, and there's nothing wrong with that. But saying you have to move is a terrible recipe that will get rocks thrown at you in many towns, and deservedly so. The structures of our economic life are not conducive to living, getting married, and having kids. I want a society where if you want to get married and have kids, the government should be there to help; that's what economic policy is all about. Commerce and markets, they're not natural states; we design them to achieve an end state which we decide as a society is better for us. But for too long, we've decided that profits are more important than children and getting married.

That needs to change.

If you live the wealthiest country in the history of the world, you shouldn't have to uproot yourself and your family to live a decent life. Should we encourage dynamism? Yes, but should we make it so if you refuse to move, you die? Hell no.

FREE-MARKETS

The American conservative movement has abandoned every value except for the value of money, profit, and markets. The right needs a fundamental rethinking of what we are even doing here. What are our goals? Who is the economy meant to serve? These basic questions have to be rethought. It shouldn't be radical for me to say that we have some values other than profit-making.

The neoliberals, who are free-market fundamentalists, the free-market is always good, but the total free-market ideology is a fraud. It's really just a cover for the financial industry that caused the 2008 stock market crash, where no one went to jail or was blamed, and that blindly got $4 trillion immediately when the economy shut down in spring of 2020 while politicians in Congress balked at giving a few hundred dollars to ordinary citizens.

The current economic theory of the right, the supply-side economics of the Reagan era, is dead. We live in a different world now, with a radically different economy. Going back to that zombie Reaganism, reusing the same old plays that don't consider the impacts of China's integration into the global economy, is not going to get us the same results as they did then. We have to face reality as it is, not how we wish it were.

I'm not a socialist by any measure, but I don't think it's a compelling argument to "own the libs" by celebrating the big corporations that hate us, censor us, and hollow out our country for a few bucks. That type of thinking is held by the Chamber of Commerce, the Cato Institute, and the libertarian elite, who are completely out of place in the Republican Party and would do better to join the Democrats, which is now the party of off-shoring, free-trade, and low-wage immigration.

This free-market enthusiasm of the Republican elite makes economic policy too central, relying on it to solve social problems and shape policy. Even what we consider to be the free-market is an illusion; an actual free-market would have the ability for market failure, but we seem to be unable to let people and companies fail. We constantly bail out corporations and industries that aren't fit to continue to survive, then don't move a muscle while wages for average workers are stagnant, as workers are charged two and a half times more now for education, housing, and healthcare than they were 30 years ago.

The market is one of many social institutions that aggregate our knowledge and allow us to improve ourselves by enabling people to make choices in their own lives. The reason that it works is not that choice itself is the most important thing, but that we know so little on the whole that we have to allow knowledge to be aggregated through individual choice. But the market itself is not the end-all-be-all.

I worry that if the right continues to adhere to the Nikki Haley or the Paul Ryan view that trying to do anything about our problems is bad, we'll lose to people who will do something about our problems. We need to be more assertive in offering a positive vision and think about public policy's role in moving us toward it because individual freedom alone does not trump our obligation to others.

We need to return to the idea that we put our population at the center of our policy and understand that the true benefit of your life does not come down to how much GDP is growing. It's about your family and putting policies into place so you can live a successful and meaningful life with as many kids as you want to have and live wherever you want to live. An actual conservative solution to economics is to put constraints on the market, constrain immigration, and reduce environmental regulation—to get an economy that works for people, not companies.

For all those neoliberals who are in uproar and are saying, "What are you talking about? Our nation is a free-market!" I only have this response: The United States doesn't have a free-market economy, it has a market economy. The government interferes all the time on behalf of corporations and the investor class. And our economic model is broken.

The fixes I'd like to see aren't about punishing companies by raising corporate taxes; it's about getting the people who have the power to admit there is a problem and acknowledge their solutions have not worked. It's not enough to mess around the edges; the government has to lead, not follow corporations.

I do think the market economy is the best system of economics in practice, but there is a weird and strange obsession of many on the right that elevates the free-market above all. The free-market is not an end in itself, but it's an end to be used and harnessed to make life more comfortable for our people, grow our might, and make it easier for people to get married and form families. That is the issue with neoliberalism: it is so focused on the individual that it makes people forget that families and the community at large are what allow society to operate efficiently.

Which is why right needs to remain committed to capitalism but also recognize that it's a system that requires rules. For the actual economic arrangements, if we want them to serve and advance a flourishing nation, the market will not do that by itself. In finding solutions that make the market work better, right-wing liberals are going to have just to admit that markets don't always work well.

TRADE

The attitude, rhetorically at least, of the Trump administration toward trade and tariffs seems to be the correct one for the times. Alliances can shift at any time, but trying to micromanage the economy, as the progressive left would have us do, is bad for the country and is actually the cause of the disparity between people. As the Covid-19 pandemic showed us, we need to focus on the need to keep our supply chains in American hands.

Since the end of World War II, the United States and most of the developed world have followed a free-trade policy between nations. Such trade was promised to bring nations together, lessen the chances of another world war, and reduce the cost of goods. It's not a flawed theory, and considering the advances made in the last several decades, it may deliver on at least some of the promises given. But setting that aside, the fact is that there are more wars now than before, and people have forgotten the enormous growth of the United States economy under the protectionist scheme.

Protectionism is not the boogeyman given by today's economists but the structuring of a nation's trade policy to protect its national sovereignty, ensure its economic self-reliance, and prosper America first. It was the policy of the Republicans from Abraham Lincoln to Calvin Coolidge. America began that era in 1860 with one-half of Britain's production and ended it by producing more than all of Europe put together. It put the economic health of the nation first. The only way to defend against cheap production, low wages, and a low standard of living that exists outside of our country and maintain our own standards of living is through a protective tariff.

The right used to believe in protection as a national policy, with due and equal regard to all sections and to all classes, and the base seems to be returning to that position. A protective tariff is designed to support the high American economic level of life for the average family and to prevent a lowering of the level of economic life to that prevailing in other lands. It is only by adherence to such a policy that the well-being of consumers can be safeguarded and that there can be assured to American agriculture, American labor, and American manufacturers a return to perpetuate American standards of living.

In our nation's history, the protective tariff system has always justified itself by restoring confidence, promoting industrial activity and employment, enormously increasing our purchasing power, and bringing increased prosperity to all our people. The tariff protection for our industry works for increased consumption of domestic agricultural products by an employed population instead of one unable to purchase the necessities of life. Without the strict maintenance of the tariff principle, our farmers will always need to compete with cheap lands and cheap labor abroad and with lower living standards.

In theory, higher tariffs on imports plus lower corporate taxes at home should have produced a boom in capital spending and domestic production. In reality, however, investment remained anemic throughout the Trump presidency, especially when compared to similar periods of full employment, and a broad-based domestic manufacturing rebound never materialized.

Why not?

In my view, Trump's tariff–tax cut combination failed to boost domestic production, primarily because tariffs are far more effective at protecting existing industries than at developing new (or lost) ones. The depleted U.S. industrial base is more in need of the latter. Thus, while tariffs likely did encourage some additional investment in the steel sector, for example, they were unlikely to encourage the rebuilding of hollowed-out sectors such as telecom equipment manufacturing, flat-panel displays, lithium-ion batteries, heavy forgings, advanced machine tools, laser diodes, drone hardware, active pharmaceutical ingredients, and on and on.

Developing advanced manufacturing industries—and, specifically, competing with the Asian manu-facturing model—requires a much more robust set of supporting policies aside from trade barriers, such as investment subsidies, supply chain mapping, shared production facilities, process innovation support, and sources of stable demand (i.e., government procure-ment). The Trump administration was too often absent on all of these issues.

Indeed, the administration on multiple occasions proposed cutting funding for the few programs that undertake such activities, such as the Manufacturing Extension Partnership and Manufacturing USA insti-tutes, as well as various agencies tasked with export promotion, technological research, infrastructure devel-opment, and other critical programs. The administra-tion did arrange a subsidized deal with Taiwan Semi-

conductor to build a new semiconductor foundry in
Arizona and supported a few other manufacturing projects. But nowhere did its efforts coalesce into a coordi-
nated industrial strategy.

While I want a return to a more protectionist trade
policy, almost a mercantile economy, I acknowledge that
it may not be the perfect solution, but at this point,
continuing down the same path isn't going to work,
and I'd rather we also steer clear of Marxist economics.
But if we don't acknowledge the possibility that ending
free-trade and getting away from free-market fundamentalism is a viable option, the only other choice will
be the Marxist approach. And that's dumb as hell.

OF TAXES

The best policy when it comes to taxation is one of
conservation. Our nation has resources that are beyond
computation, and if required, we would be able to meet
any challenge that faces us. But the cost of the combined
governments is likewise immense. Everyone in their
monthly bills feels this enhanced cost of existence, and
they know by experience what a burden this is on them.

The average person in this country is the one who
bears the cost of government. No matter how much the
left yells and screams, the average person is opposed to
waste. They know that government extravagance dimin-
ishes the reward for their labor and, plainly put, leaves
less money in their wallet at the end of the day. Every

dollar carelessly wasted means that their lives will be
so much more meager. Every dollar that is saved means
their lives will be so much more abundant.

In the case of my home state, Nebraska, property owners have risen up and spoken out dramatically against the property tax system, which places the
primary burden onto property owners to pay for local
government and schools.

But a sizeable group of farmers and ranchers
recently attempted to place a constitutional amendment
before voters that would give an income tax credit equal
to 35% of the property taxes paid. Such a plan is an
entirely asinine and overly complex method. Instead of
reducing the need for so much in tax dollars by local
governments, their solution was to force the state to pay
the difference...somehow.

The solutions in recent years to give tax relief that
has passed the Nebraska legislature has been to provide
refunds or tax credits, in short, make the tax code
much more complicated and open for abuses by special
deals. Republicans pushing for such things loses us the
trust of the voters and gives the Democrats' outlandish
complaints some basis in truth. It is an entirely unforced
error on our part and one that can be easily avoided.

The soundest way to solve tax problems in any
locality or state is through cutting spending. There are
many programs that the government does not need to
be at the center of. The collection of any taxes which
are not absolutely required and which do not beyond

reasonable doubt contribute to the public welfare is only a form of legalized larceny. Or, in the words of Turning Point USA, taxation is theft.

In our nation, the rewards and profits of business belong to those who earn them. I know a great many socialists that have taken over the Democrat party disagree, but it's the truth. The only constitutional tax is the tax which ministers to public necessity. Not wants, but necessities. The property of a people belongs to the people. And their title to that property is absolute.

The American people do not support any privileged classes like the serfs of the Middle Ages; they ought not to be burdened with a great array of public employees who only tell them what they cannot do with their own property or that they must perform certain acts contrary to their beliefs. Whenever taxes become burdensome, a remedy can be applied by the people through their representatives; but if they do not act for themselves, no one can be very successful in acting for them.

Constant vigilance must be paid to right-wing representatives to assure that they will not fall into the trap of complacency or corruption by Democrats and lobbyists in the bubble of the state capitols. If we continue to let ourselves be fooled by representatives who claim they will reduce taxes or burdensome regulations but then do nothing but blame others for their own ineffectiveness, then we only have ourselves to blame. It is a real thing for good, well-meaning Republicans to abandon their positions when confronted with their desire to fit in and be friends with the other representatives. But the compromises they achieve are wholly on their own part and, at best, usually are nothing but the slowing down of the Democrat's own agenda.

In order for America to achieve tax reductions, unless we want to hamper the ability of the people to exercise their very right to earn a living (I am looking at you, Bernie Sanders and AOC), we must have tax reform. Most importantly, it must be properly done. Raising money for the government should not impede the transaction of business but encourage it. The correct course to follow in taxation and all other economic legislation is not to destroy those who have already secured success but to create conditions under which everyone will have a better chance to succeed.

Extremely high tax rates, such as those proposed by the extreme far left who run the Democrat Party now, raise only a little to no revenue because they are bad for the country and because they are wrong. What person would be willing to work hard and put in long hours to earn money only for the government to take most of the reward for their labor? The correct answer is none! They would rather work less, be less industrious, be less innovative.

We cannot finance the country, and we cannot improve social conditions through any system of injustice, even if we inflict it upon the rich. It is nothing new, but Democrats like Alexandria Ocasio-Cortez or Nancy

Pelosi pretend that this time, things will be different. This time, it will work.

But those who will suffer the most harm will be the poor. We have seen this story play out time after time all throughout the world and throughout time.

CONCLUSION

Reshoring American supply chains makes us safer in the long run, from an economic perspective, a national security perspective, and a public health perspective. A great nation makes things for itself. There is a real benefit to being able to make things in America. Just because it's cheaper, the alter of globalization, the alter of cheap prices, has made us make horrific political choices over the last four decades, and going on that and praying towards that alter has made us less safe, less robust.

Everything has been used to justify those ends, and it hasn't made us happy, it hasn't made us satisfied, it hasn't brought us any sort of spiritual nourishment or community, and community is something we have completely dispatched with and devalued in the country as well.

Markets have been providing a lot of GDP growth and delivering a lot of absolute wealth, but in terms of widespread prosperity and providing a foundation where people of all aptitudes and all places can build good lives, the market has not been delivering as it needs to or as we expect it to for quite a while. Libertarians aren't concerned with market outcomes; they see the market itself as an end, and more liberty is the end of the discussion. Conservatives love markets and markets are exactly the right way we should be organizing the private sector of our society, and we need a large, robust private sector, I'm not going to take for granted that whatever markets are doing is great.

Markets are a construct that needs to operate within a set of rules to deliver outcomes that support strong families and communities above all else. When they are not doing that, it is absolutely important and conservative to say, "Well, why not? What do we need to change?"

For a long time, conservatives have outsourced all of that economic thinking to libertarians, to the point that we now think that tax cuts, deregulation, free trade, that's conservative. But none of those things are inherently conservative.

CHAPTER SEVEN

THE ENVIRONMENT

The right usually messes things up whenever it comes to environmental matters. That's a result of our natural inclination to conserve things getting distorted by right-wing liberal talking points that say beauty doesn't have a value, so it's irrelevant.

Beauty in the natural world is terribly important, and too many people these days forget that. Sure, everyone will acknowledge, however reluctantly, the beauty of America's national parks and natural wonders such as the Grand Tetons, Monument Valley, the Great Smokey Mountains, or Niagara Falls. Still, many seem to overlook the massive ranches of the west, the mile

after mile of row-crops and pastureland, and the small
towns with weathered signs that dot the landscape, all
of which are, in their own way, sublime.

Too many want to pave over the fields, remove what
was there, in favor of a cookie-cutter design of concrete
and glass strip malls and manicured grass, and call that
progress. That is not progress; it is wanton destruction
of what makes a place unique.

Telling people that their way of life, the way they
and their families have used the land over generations,
is wrong and that the enlightened few, who barely know
anything about the land they are talking about, say only
they know what's best, not the farmers and ranchers
who depend on that land.

This is where the right can take back the issue of
the environment and get the public at large to care
about preserving and conserving the environment. Any
environmental policy put forward by the right needs to
respect the people's sentiments of national identity as
part of a humane and inclusive patriotism designed to
unite the generations in defense of our shared ecological inheritance.

The natural skepticism of humanity would serve us
well here. Most environmental problems occur when
the natural homeostatic systems break down, and the
government's intervention, no matter how well-intentioned, can be a significant cause of disequilibrium
in nature. What makes matters worse, other than our
inability to actually solve the problem, is that the free-

market ceases to deliver solutions to environmental issues when it can externalize their costs, escape the internal rules of the system, and wash it's hands of having to do anything about what they did. With, of course, the government's blessing.

So, if you're going to claim you're a conservative, then certain realities that deal with the environment have to be dealt with. You can't stick your fingers in your ears and yell, "I can't hear you!" anytime the topic is even raised.

We have to support conserving the natural beauty of the United States, not the bulldozing of our natural wonders for parking lots and big-box stores that only destroy the main streets of our towns. We must maintain America's natural beauty for future generations. And that means dealing with climate change.

CLIMATE CHANGE

Whenever a topic like climate change is brought up, the right has a reflex to automatically dismiss whatever is said. I don't think it's because we're climate deniers or anything like that; it's just that we on the right have been trained by years of experience to disbelieve anything the elites and the left have told us.

I, for one, believe that climate change is happening, and humanity may be playing a role in it, but the solutions presented by the left are entirely unrealistic.

Climate change is a natural occurrence; the climate, by definition, changes. And humanity's presence on Earth does affect things, but questions pop up when the left tries to pin the blame solely on human behavior.

No matter how much we do, there is no keeping the temperature of the Earth static; not unless we start killing off the human and animal populations wholesale, which really isn't up for discussion. In the meantime, we are told to give up modern life while other nations that are the most significant drivers of carbon emissions and outright pollution are ignored.

Over the last ten years, the United States has reduced its emissions more than the following 12 countries combined. Even without the massive carbon taxes the left proposes, America is doing its part, but you won't hear that from the fear-mongers. All we hear is that we must cut carbon emissions, that there has to be a carbon tax with corporate offsets (so they can still pollute), and all these bureaucratic messes to govern how ordinary people live their lives. It's all rubbish.

I think we are very capable of taking care of our own little patches of Earth without the fascist pollution police instructing us on how we're all messing everything up.

Climate change isn't seen as an issue to discuss but an issue to fight each other about. We are all egged on by the left in horrific ways.

When people are told not to associate with family members who disagree, you aren't dealing with politics anymore; you're dealing with a cult. When you're told to give up your worldly goods, to remove yourself from the environment of your family and loved ones if they do not sufficiently believe in the correct view, that is a cult.

Meanwhile, our children are being brainwashed into this cult in our schools by being told that we adults are destroying the environment and that anyone who wants to discuss solutions that are anything but what the left says are evil and wrong.

The whole matter of climate change has acquired all the hallmarks of a left-wing cause. There is a class of victims, the future generations; an enlightened vanguard fighting for those victims against the powerful philistines who exploit them; but most importantly, there are endless opportunities to express resentment against the successful, the wealthy, and Western society overall.

However, climate change shouldn't be a left-wing cause. Rather than liberating or empowering victims to overthrow the bourgeoise swine, it's really about safeguarding our resources, conservation, and equilibrium.

It's crucial for the climate change activists on the left to use fear for political ends, to destroy national sovereignty, and exert top-down control by the self-appointed experts over the ordinary activities of mankind. Constant catastrophism is their primary weapon; if we indeed were in a climate emergency, we would have seen people behave as people did during the first weeks of the coronavirus pandemic. But we don't. People go around living their lives as usual, not like there was an emergency.

Admittedly, I am not an expert in this field, but what I have been able to gather is that coal-fired power plants are seen as the largest emitters of carbon dioxide into the Earth's atmosphere; hence so many of the environmental left's plans call for solar and wind power to replace them. But those systems alone cannot provide the necessary energy required, and battery capacity is nowhere near ready to make solar or wind viable on the required scale.

If the left was serious about cutting carbon emissions, the solution is obvious: more nuclear power stations. The only other alternative is to develop commercial fusion reactors or other advanced technologies that aren't real yet. If the left wants to handle climate change issues, then they have to propose solutions other than a massive tax grab for "reasons."

Of course, climate change is a major issue that we must address if we can, but it is a global issue that lies mainly beyond the reach of small nations and the communities that are protected by them. It is far more important to ensure that we settle on this planet in ways that do not damage it and that harmonize humanity with nature.

Ultimately, the general problem with environmental politics is the clash between the top-down view of government and the bottom-up procedures of democratic choice. The changes that have put climate change

at the top of the environmental agenda have also under-
mined the status of democracy: people complaining
of planning blight and spoliation are dismissed out of
hand as NIMBYs, and all projects can be swept aside for
the sake of the "climate emergency".

And it's the use of the word "emergency" that is
revealing here. In emergencies, we surrender our powers
to the common cause and put the state in charge of them.
That is what we are being invited to do in all matters
relating to the environment, so that our real resources in
dealing with those matters—most notably our sense of
beauty and our love of place—can be discounted.

SUBURBIA

The most important man-made environmental
problem in America is the spread of the suburbs. Suburbanization causes the increasing use of automobiles, and
the dispersal of populations in ways that exponentially
raise the consumption of energy and non-degradable
packaging. Disingenuous politicians on the right argue
that this is a result of freedom and the market, that
people settle outside the towns because that is what they
want. They are moving out in search of green fields,
wooded gardens, tranquility—in short, their own little
patch of nature. But this is not so.

They are not moving out in search of a natural
environment but in search of a suburban environment,
and they are doing so because the suburban environ-

ment is massively subsidized by the state. The roads, the infrastructure, and the schools—all state invest ments—which entirely imbalance the natural economy of the town, and make it easier, safer, and cheaper to live on the edge of it—an edge that is constantly moving further from the city center, thus destroying the advantages offered to those who move to the suburbs just a year after they move.

The mechanism here is not a free market mechanism. Much of the expansion of the suburbs is proceeded by the exercise of "eminent domain"—that provision in American law which gives the official bodies powers equal to, and sometimes exceeding, the powers exerted by the socialist governments of Europe.

Roads are one obvious instance of this, and the mania for building them in order to maintain traffic flows at a level arbitrarily imposed by official bodies, is the most important cause of the reckless mobility of American society. The true market solution to the problem of traffic congestion—which is to get out of your car and walk—is not available in America since most of the time there is no way that you could walk to your destination. Be it the shop, the church, the school, or just your nearest friend, suburbanization has put your goal beyond pedestrian reach.

But we cannot live in the center of the cities any more either. The elites complain: they're not safe. Downtown is for bums and drop-outs; the schools are appalling, the crime-rate soaring, and the place rife with drugs, alcohol, and prostitution. Well yes, that's exactly what happens when the state subsidizes the suburbs, imposes zoning laws that prevent proper mixed use in the towns, and engages in its own gargantuan housing projects that drive the middle classes out of the city centers. All this occurs in defiance of the market solution and, as Jane Jacobs pointed out in 1965, in *The Death and Life of Great American Cities*, it deprives the city of its eyes and its ears, of its close communities and natural fellowship.

I mention this example not only because it illustrates how far environmental damage has advanced and how difficult it will be to rectify it, but also because it illustrates two rather more important points: first, the mistaken view that it is the market, and not the state, that has created the problem; and secondly, the equally mistaken view that the environment can be discussed without raising questions of beauty.

In my view, problems arise precisely when we interrupt the normal ways in which people solve their problems by free interaction. In other words, the problems come from expropriating the paths of rational consensus—as they are expropriated by the state whenever it uses its powers of eminent domain. And the solutions come when we allow our sense of beauty and place to take over, aiming at what looks right, what feels right, and what we can vindicate in the eyes and hearts of our neighbors.

American cities have decayed because vast tax-funded resources have been available for the building of roads and housing projects; for the purchase and demolition of otherwise habitable street-based neighborhoods condemned as slums; for the horizontal spread of infrastructure; and for the imposition of crazy zoning laws which ensure that where you can buy things you cannot do things, and where you can do things you cannot live. And the solutions to these problems emerge when people, constrained by the natural limitations posed by the need to reach consensual solutions and without the gargantuan schemes of officialdom, set about building a neighborhood that looks right to those who live in it, and which is welcoming to those who buy and sell and work.

The left is mistaken when it takes the view that it is just the market, not the state, that creates environmental issues. And the right needs to keep in mind that the idea that the environment can be discussed without raising questions of beauty is a total fallacy. We need to keep the beauty of our natural world in mind, not just the abstract figures and concepts.

CONSERVATION

The whole matter of not just climate change, but environmentalism itself, is a conservative cause, for it is the absolute most vivid instance of the partnership between the dead, the living, and the unborn that Edmund Burke talks about. It makes common sense as well; through a shared love of our home and its customs, we are called to account not just to those around us but also to past and future generations. We may have title to the land and nature around us, but in truth, we are merely trustees charged with its maintenance.

Only the private ownership of land confers responsibility for the environment, and that is not the same as the unqualified right to exploit it, as the socialists the world over have done, both historically and currently. But to get the people at large to care about preserving and conserving the environment, any environmental policy put forward by conservatives needs to respect the people's sentiments of national identity as a part of a humane and inclusive patriotism and be designed to unite the generations in defense of our shared ecological inheritance.

Even among the right these days, words like trust, settlement, beauty, and home are looked down upon as old-fashioned sentiments that can be easily disregarded with a wave of the hand by those in positions of power and influence. It makes me wonder why, when we talk about those things, is the discussion determined by those whose preferred solutions involve the total destruction of the things we love? We have to have conversations openly and honestly, and I'm afraid that most of the left, and many on the right, will not agree to that. As trustees of the Earth, we owe it to our ancestors and our unborn descendants to thoughtfully and carefully manage it, not act hysterically.

The eminent Sir Roger Scruton believed that vital to the conservative environmental movement is the love of beauty, seeing it as a shared resource. The idea of beauty, he wrote, acted as a barrier to the top-down brutalities of the exploiters and social engineers who littered the landscape with wind farms, not because there was any scientific authority for it, but because it refocused the problem into a global one, rather than a local or national one.

I think the environmental left is on to something about the planet, but its problem is that it keeps showing its true neo-Marxist core and its desire not to build a better relationship between ourselves and the natural world around us, but the total end of capitalism. And that makes it incredibly difficult for anybody on the right to discuss what we should be doing.

So when anybody comes along and says, "I think there's a problem so bad that you're going to have to spend everything and end the best system of growth that has ever been found by mankind, a system of growth that has taken half of the people on the planet out of extreme poverty in this century and the last, but this problem is so severe that you have to crash that system of growth you have," then I would like to discuss that.

I don't want to take them at their word for it. I don't want to be blackmailed into making that decision. But blackmail is what the environmental left is demanding.

SOLUTIONS

The differences between conservatives and radical environmentalists are vast. We conservatives value the cultural and political traditions we have inherited from the past. Being conservationists, we value our ecological heritage and desire to pass it along, undiminished, to our descendants. Meanwhile, the radical environmentalists are quite comparable to the communists of the 20th century. They believe the capitalist world to be corrupt and want to sweep away all its vestiges in the name of something new. Similarly, radical environmentalists see our technological domination of the natural world so harshly that they want to destroy it and institute completely new principles.

Finally, the centralized bureaucracies meant to deal with pollution and the environment are entirely useless. The Environmental Protection Agency of the United States displaced local associations with a professional, rule-bound bureaucracy with an incentive structure completely unrelated to improving particular places and instead has a one-size-fits-all set of rules that are perversely irrelevant or counterproductive in the field.

The most stunning example of such incompetence was the EPA's inability to accept the Dutch offer of pollution-abatement ships during the 2010 Deepwater Horizon oil spill in the Gulf of Mexico due to the fact that the Dutch ships did not meet the impossibly high standard of decontaminating seawater to a 99.5% purity level. Ships that could've helped remove vast quantities of crude oil, that have done so in the North Sea, were rejected because of the very slightly contaminated water they would have disgorged back into the sea.

There is also a massive temptation by conservatives and Republicans to embrace a comprehensive plan, similar to the progressives' Green New Deal. But that would still be a statist solution, threatening not only individual liberty but also the ability for consensual solutions to emerge. A top-down, imposed from above solution, often leaves them without the ability to course-correct and are hardly reversed when there is proof of failure. This inflexibility goes hand in hand with the progressive's planned and goal-directed nature. And when these plans fail, the government will not change them, but instead gaslight the public into believing they haven't failed.

However, governments don't easily admit mistakes they've made, and so the official propaganda continues to speak as though the wind farms were the lasting proof of environmental rectitude. An example of this is the ruination of the Dutch and Danish coastal landscapes by banks of wind farms. They stand looming on the horizon of the sea, blighting the landscape. But people put up with them because they have been told that they are the solution to depleted energy sources. Yet, they don't produce very much power and will never be able to take the place of coal or nuclear power plants in being able to provide the baseload that the nation requires.

There is no simple or straightforward solution, so I'm going to repeat what I said earlier: that humans do contribute to climate change, but we are one of many sources of greenhouse gases. We should reduce greenhouse gases where possible, but not at the expense of other worthwhile projects. The left's plans for large-scale attempts to micromanage the world's economy to mitigate carbon emissions are unlikely to make us wealthier in the long run. In fact, the best models show that any realistic carbon tax will make us poorer, not richer.

So, we should oppose every large-scale, government-run, or corporate-run carbon mitigation plan, including those being pushed by Republicans. It would be better to do nothing than accept the left's favored option, so why take a left-lite option instead?

At the same time, we need to accept that the discovery of a breakthrough technology may never happen, so our best option as humans might be to adapt to a slightly warmer world. That isn't to say we throw our hands in the air and give up; even small things such as planting trees and painting roofs in cities with reflective paint have been shown to cool urban areas significantly. In short, we should act where we can, and it's prudent to do so. If you are really looking for a way to reduce carbon emissions, then the only answer is to replace coal-fired power plants with next-generation nuclear power.

The truth is that there are still many unknowns surrounding climate change. We don't know how much the world will warm; projections have been wildly inaccurate so far. We don't know how it'll affect our day-to-day well-being. All we can do is estimate the economic and ecological costs and speculate wildly about future technology. The proper response to a future we don't know is to build upon what we do know. And I know that the true answer to climate change will not come from a massive new tax plan.

It is questionable at best to argue that large-scale attempts to manage the economy and mitigate carbon emissions will make us wealthier in the long run. The best models show that any realistic carbon tax—or worse, any set of command-and-control regulations or any crony-capitalist carbon-credit auction scheme—will make us poorer, not richer. The first rule of conservative policymaking is to do no harm. Conservatives should oppose every large-scale, government-run carbon-mitigation plan, including the carbon tax that some on the right, like former congressman Bob Inglis, have hailed. Rigorous examination shows it would be better to do nothing than to accept the progressives' favored options.

Conservatives, however, should not limit themselves to merely opposing the Waxman-Markey plan in Congress. They can champion an agenda that understands human beings to be much more imaginative than the economic models expect. By fostering the legal and economic ecosystems most conducive to breakthrough energy technologies, conservatives can help lessen the harm of climate change. As stated above, this includes property rights and a modest regulatory state that allow would-be innovators to learn through trial and error.

The second priority should be the kinds of public policies that actually help foster innovation. Investment in general infrastructure—both classic projects, like roads and bridges, and newer ones, in the area of digital infrastructure—greases the economic wheels. We also need to invest in visionary technologies that are too long-term, too speculative, or have benefits too diffuse to be funded by private companies.

During the 1980s and 1990s, the Department of Energy drastically increased its micromanagement of its labs in response to Congressional pressure to reduce waste and increase safety. This removed responsibility for core operating decisions, including personnel, travel, and project management, from the contractors that operate the labs to the DOE itself. That has greatly constrained the ability of the labs to flexibly pursue new innovations. The labs should be returned to a more independent, contractor-led model with clearer goals but greater operational flexibility. We might, for example, set one lab the goal of driving the true unit-cost of energy produced by a solar cell below that of coal, and for a second lab, the same task for nuclear power.

At least one lab should be devoted to the geo-engineering technologies that can remove carbon dioxide from the atmosphere or mollify its heating effects. There is no reason why we should seek only technologies that lower our carbon use when the real goal is to avoid the damaging effects of a much warmer world. Because it tries to "engineer" a system we know very little about, geo-engineering should be pursued with utmost prudence and held in reserve as a "break glass in case of emergency" option.

All of these proposed policies build upon successes. When it comes to climate change, the right need not theorize about conspiracies or hide behind ignorance. We should confront the facts as scientists generally understand them, as well as the limits of that understanding, and we should seek to empower innovators looking for solutions.

The answer to the complex question of climate change will be neither a regulatory Rube Goldberg machine nor a massive new tax. Rather, conservatives should champion what they so frequently suggest as the best way to solve complex problems: policies that open the space for the private sector to innovate and adapt.

CHAPTER EIGHT

SOCIETY

The reason why every institution is against traditional American values is that the conservatives of the past, as well as those today, were too scared to control these institutions due to their anti-big government dogma. Those free-market obsessed neoliberals who talk about limiting government power are trying to limit the last tool the right has to express power in our society; we don't have economic power or cultural power, the last thing we have is governmental power. We must wield the power of the state when we have it, or we will be crushed.

We must use economic means for conservative ends. But the structures of our economic life today are not conducive to living, getting married, and having kids.

I want a society where if you want to get married and have kids, the government should be there to help; that's what economic policy should be all about. Commerce and markets, what neoliberals hold most dear, are not natural states; they're designed by us to achieve an end state that we decide as a society is better for us. So, we should use them accordingly.

For too long, the right has decided that profits are more important than children and getting married. Because of that, we're not doing a good job of ensuring that everybody in our culture is getting the goods and skills to compete in our meritocracy. The stupid way of fixing that is trying to build parallel institutions, the path taken by most conservative elites.

The American dream is about having a good job, raising your family, and saying what you want to say about the direction of this country, and all of those things are being threatened by the corporate oligarchy.

One of the biggest difficulties in our time is that conservative leaders have come to look upon society, vaguely, as a homogeneous mass of identical individuals whose happiness may be obtained by direction from above, through legislation or some scheme of public instruction. We should endeavor to teach humanity once more that the germ of public affection (in Burke's words) is "to learn to love the little platoon we belong to in society."

Social liberalization has had a sinister impact on our society, producing a society of atomized consumers with little concern for the good of their families, communities, or nation. John Gray's critique of Mill's harm principle, the idea that the individual can do whatever they wish so long as it does not "harm" anyone. But this view often papers over the subtler yet equally consequential social costs associated with self-harm.

Drug legalization or decriminalization is a case in point. Every drug addict has a family and a community that are also harmed by their behavior, be it through the immense pain of the loss of a loved one or by the economic burden of supporting drug addiction, all of which is masked by the harm principle and its individualistic assumptions.

The emerging drug consensus, in terms of a libertine social agenda that ties back to identity politics, is pushed at the complete behest and benefit of big business. It's ultimately a bottom-line benefit for Goldman Sachs and venture capital firms that are advocating to reduce FDA regulation and their ability to have insight into mind-altering substances with 40% THC. Running an experiment on millions of young and developing brains all towards a cultural agenda of so-called freedom is a good way to get people addicted and hooked on substances in order to deal with the miserable economic conditions that govern their lives.

In viewing freedom in terms of an individual's right to dispose of their own life however they wish, as long as they cause no physical harm to others (i.e. drug decriminalization), ignores the interconnection of all human lives and the harm to society of viewing citizens as nothing more than atomized individuals pursuing only their own happiness. These two approaches are inextricably bound together: economic individualism begets social atomization and vice versa; together they lead only to social disintegration and the collapse of any bonds of community or shared identity.

But, right now, conservative politics is all about economics and how much government intervention there's going to be. As soon as you talk about religion and nationalist things, people give you economic answers. For example, the opioid crisis, we need an economic answer to that. God and scripture are disappearing from even conservative areas, so the answer given for that is charter schools.

Economics alone will not solve these problems. We need a political theory that takes human beings as they are. That means we have to recognize there's such a thing as cohesion, familial and tribal bonds.

The survival and flourishing of the state depend upon its citizens' willingness to put the interests of the community before their own. In the continental conservative tradition, the unity of the community is understood in terms of values, beliefs, and ideals. For example, to be a Frenchman and a citizen, you do not have to be born in France but subscribe to certain central tenets about the proper way of living in and serving French society.

Within the political elites, there may be division and dissent, but the plurality of opinions expressed by average Americans are expected to be expressed as differences in how to achieve the central mission of the state. Instead, it must be understood as the product, not of institutions or ideals, but of "a long and messy story that takes in our history, our shared stories, and our collective experiences," a "reverence of particular places" and of a particular culture, all amounting to a collective national identity. If anyone can enjoy the rights of citizenship within a political community without the obligations to the community it confers, then citizenship becomes meaningless.

We have to reorient our economic life and economic policies towards incentivizing the building of communities and the building of institutions that exist outside of just the direct check from the government or the direct check from your workforce. It needs to be about unions, higher wages, and the strength of families.

People will put up with a lot of crap, and they will persist and will invest in the community, invest in their lives, and invest in a productive civil society if they feel that life will get better for themselves and their kids. But the core breakdown is that people no longer have that confidence. People want to get married still, they just can't afford to. And that for their kids, they're not going to have it better than they had.

When you lose that hope, that's when things go off the rails.

SOCIAL CONTRACT

We need a new conservatism. A restoration of the old orders of morality, religion, institutions, and virtues. The social contract is not just between us here and now, but with us as individuals, the unborn, those who have come before, and God. Natural rights are universal truths from the Almighty and cannot be defined by mere mortals in a single document, no matter how long and comprehensive we believe it to be. In the eyes of the law and justice, everyone is the same, but at the same time, we recognize that we do not have the same talents, abilities, and characteristics. That we are each unique.

The social contract, a concept many of us learned in school, needs to have an expanded understanding. Most parties to that contract are either dead or not yet born. To forget this, to throw away customs and institutions just because you think they are outdated, is to place the members of society living right now in a dictatorial dominance over those who went before and those who came after them. This is why conservatives should seek to protect these things against those who would tear them down out of a misguided zeal for what they see as

the demands of liberty, equality, social justice, or even
the free market.

Neoliberalism is not a term that Rousseau would
use, nor would he recognize his ideas in those thinkers
whom we now describe as classical liberals. Liberalism
is an intellectual tradition, formed from the interplay
of two political ideals: liberty and equality. Liberals
differ according to whether liberty or equality is more
important to them. Libertarians believe that liberty
should be traded for nothing else save liberty, whereas
the present-day American neoliberal tends to sacrifice
liberty for equality when the two conflict.

Both libertarians and egalitarians are hostile to
vested authority, and this hostility unites the two in
practice, even if it is hard to reconcile them in theory.
Rousseau cared passionately for both liberty and
equality. But he also brought to the fore some of the
deep tensions between them. He observed with disgust
what people did with their freedom; and this disgust
was proof of the deep inequality that distinguished him
from so many of his contemporaries.

And I tend to believe Burke was right about the
"little platoon". Those small subdivisions in society
include your family, neighborhood, church, or clubs.
This is where we all live. This is our practical everyday
life. Instead of focusing on the big national events, we
need to look at each other on this lower, more basic
level of society. This is where we work together, where
we build relationships, where we find happiness. And

without certain values such as morality, religion, solidity, property, peace, order, and manners; liberty has little benefit and will not last.

The American conservative movement has been a complete disaster for America so far. Their answer against collectivism (progressivism and neo-Marxism) being individualism means that on one side the collectivists are destroying organic institutions and social capital while the individualists are also destroying institutions and social capital by arguing against collective action. Both sides are effectively in a pincer move, destroying the fundamental basics of American society.

As much as the left wishes it were so, there cannot be just scientific solutions to societal problems. People's lives are much deeper than that. The free-market enthusiasm of the modern right makes economic policy too central, relying on it too much to solve social problems and shape policy. But nothing is more fundamental than the dignity of the human person; but to flourish, people need relationships, beginning with the family.

FAMILIES

A society isn't defined by its gross domestic product or its capacity to sell endless vice and consumerism; it is defined by its people, culture, history, and heritage. And the bedrock of that society is the family.

Unfortunately, so many politicians on the right like to tout their support of family values while supporting a corporatist regime that has crushed American families by destroying local small businesses, promoting extremist groups like Black Lives Matter and Antifa to erase American history, and going along with re-writing the very definition of man and woman.

We need to ask what it is conservatives are actually trying to conserve. If it's a traditional way of life for most people born in the United States, we have to recognize that it has clearly eroded over the last 30 years. So much so that, for the first time in modern history, we live in a time when parents know with relative certainty that, on average, their kids will not be as well off as they were at the same age. Add in the structural barriers ranging from student loan debt to lack of job mobility in their hometowns cripple their ability to live a "normal" life.

The key part of living the traditional American way of life is marriage. I know of many libertarians who say that the government shouldn't be involved in marriage at all, mainly to avoid saying that they agree with gay marriage in very conservative areas of the country. But marriage is pre-political. It existed long before our government, even western civilization.

Yet, I believe that the government needs to be involved in marriage because it affirms what is a part of the backbone of society: families and marriage. Society has a vested interest in marriages because they create those families that form the backbone of society. More importantly, we need couples to stay together to have a healthy, prosperous relationship so that their children, who are the future of our society, are raised well.

Strong families, not GDP growth, are the backbone of American society. Of every society. But for all of the economic growth our country has had, American society is broken today. Across America, birth rates have fallen. Children born now are exponentially more likely to be born out-of-wedlock than even 20 years ago. Marriages have slowed even during the COVID-19 pandemic, and divorces are still high. Family formation is discouraged, and abortions are promoted because the American elite hates the family, hates tradition, and frankly hates the American people.

I would say that the right should care about declining fertility not just because it's bad for our economy but because we think babies are good, and we think babies are good because we're not sociopaths.

The Republican Party's focus on paid formal labor as the only kind of valuable work and the dismissal of parenting as valuable work is wrong. We need to make it so a family can survive on a single income. The right and left overstate the value of paid labor and understate the value of parenting. Encouraging this will help people have more children, raising our birth and fertility rates.

The conservative establishment has verbally touted "family values" for decades. Yet they've supported the globalist regime that has crushed American families. We're here to build a conservative movement that actually believes in family values. This is why I believe that we need to create policies that encourage marriages and children.

The way we got to this place in our society is very simple: in the 1960s and 1970s, there was a push from various sources to get more women into the workforce. As more women entered the workforce, their children still had to be looked after. Enter daycare. As time went on, women were encouraged to put their careers first, just like men, and if they did get married and have a family, they weren't given promotions or raises at the same rate as men.

This started a cycle of more women putting off having families, lowering the birth rate, and so on and so on. When women did have children, they had fewer than they may have wanted due to the cost of daycare, which they couldn't afford without working, causing them to decide to have fewer children. This is the spiral we are in, and I don't think anybody will like where we are headed.

This just speaks to the problem of the current conservative establishment. When they espouse family values, they should actually mean family values instead of supporting large corporations that are now asking women to freeze their eggs to remain employees longer. That should be a choice for women to make without the implied threat that they and their families won't be able to afford a decent middle-class life if they want to have a kid. This really isn't rocket science: some women don't

want to have kids or are unable to have kids, but some
women do want to have more kids, or kids at all.

This drop in fertility has happened in every single
nation that has developed, starting with the UK and
then the US, and proceeding on through western
Europe, southern and eastern Europe, Japan, China, and
now into India. Each went through an S-shaped population curve, where population growth first skyrocketed
as infant mortality dropped, then reached an asymptote
when women started wanting smaller families.

There is no "population bomb" waiting to go off.
The developed world is depopulating. The only popu-
lation growth is in underdeveloped countries, led by
sub-Saharan Africa, and even there, it is slowing down.
There is some evidence that much of the violence in the
Middle East was driven by declining fertility, as reli-
gious leaders realized that the prospect of outbreeding
Israel and the West was slipping from their grasp.

The only reason the US population today is rising
is because of immigration. The United States' total
fertility rate is 1.7, but a rate of 2.1 is required to
sustain a population. The only nation in the developed
world with a total fertility rate above 2.1 is Israel; all
other developed nations are not replacing their population and are declining save for immigration.

There are examples in the world that provide at
least clues on how America should establish a viable
family policy. It's very fashionable to despise Hungary,
but its pro-life and pro-family policies have successfully

reduced abortion and divorce while boosting marriage and birth rates. Their measures encourage people to have more children by taking government money and spending it directly on families. For instance, under the Hungarian system, the more children you have, the less income tax you pay, and when you have your fourth child, you get to pay no income tax for life.

Along with a host of other programs that encourage family formation, there is a program that lends young married couples 33,000 euros, and after having their third child, that loan is made into a grant that the couple doesn't have to pay back. While we can't, nor should we, directly copy Hungary's plan, it provides a guide to the types of programs and solutions available to the American right without resorting to using one of the left's watered-down plans.

I know that the left loves to talk about universal child care as the solution for working parents, but I have to ask, is that really what people want? To toil away at some crappy desk job if you're lucky, that you hate, that doesn't pay well, and with your kids being raised by someone else in their most formative years? I know I didn't enjoy doing that with my own child, and I don't believe most parents like that choice either. The American system should be set up to allow parents to choose either path. And if the conservative establishment fought for these kinds of family values as hard as they fight for corporate tax cuts, then we would all be doing better.

I worry that we have outsourced in the right parts of our economic and domestic policy thinking to libertarians. The ideas of Milton Friedman and Friedrich Hayak were very compelling in the 1960s and 1970s and still carry a lot of weight, but at a fundamental level, if we're worried about moms and dads not being as involved at home, if we're worried about rising rates of childhood trauma, if we're worried about the fact that we as a nation are not having enough children to replace ourselves, then we have to be willing to pursue a politics that actually wants to accomplish something besides just making government smaller. Sometimes government needs to be smaller, but sometimes it actually needs to work better and to work for the goals conservatives actually care about.

Predictably, neoliberals like to respond to that and say "why should we care if people are having more kids?" If you look at the economic factors, countries that have fewer children, have less innovation, have less enthusiasm, and are less stable societies. This is very fundamental mathematics because we have a social environment built around more young workers coming in to retire as senior workers, and you can't have more young people unless you have more children.

But if we suggest that, if we focus on more than economic factors, which we should be very far away from, makes us conservative. I care about declining fertility and have seen the positive role that parenthood can play in the lives of my friends and myself. I have seen young people who were less hung up, but instead rooted and grounded in their family and community because they have children.

LAW AND ORDER

The right loves to talk about law and order but doesn't really do anything about it. Even Donald Trump took a soft approach to rioting in the summer of 2020. Apart from tweets saying law and order, he didn't do a lot; he made threats to send in the national guard and even the US Army, but when the national guard did get to the scene during the riots (always at the respective governor's orders), it was always too late to stop the damage.

There's also the failure of the Trump administration and Republicans in general to challenge the basis of the over-incarceration narrative. They failed to take the opportunity to show that a lot of the people Democrats wanted to release from prison were there because that one crime you think is low level is actually their 18th crime and the one they just pled down to. But no, Trump and the Republican Party embraced criminal justice reform in the form of the First Step Act and moved the Republican Party to the left on that.

We need to restore the safety of Americans. If you want to know what path the left is taking our country down and where it leads, you just have to look at the 2020 riots. Groups of fascists, who disingenuously claim to be anti-fascists, committed mob violence in the streets in eerily similar ways to the original fascist groups in the early to mid-20th century. They tore down statues of figures such as Abraham Lincoln and U.S. Grant, who, respectively, issued the Emancipation Proclamation and led the Union to victory over the Confederacy all for the crime of not being sufficiently against the Confederacy and slavery.

These attacks by the left on historical figures do not seem to be directed against individual people but against the history of the West as a whole. It's an expression of their self-hatred that's been imbued in them since childhood in their homes, schools, media, politics, and universities, with a spirit of political correctness and a smug, know-it-all attitude. This class of people consistently gives free rein to their resentment against their own cultural identity.

For anyone who has studied the French Revolution, you know what comes next. You read about any revolution, and you'll know what comes next. To superimpose a societal structure from the outside or recreate it from the inside, you have to destroy the past first. You have to destroy all the institutions that have held up that society so far. This is what the left has been doing not just to America but to the entire West.

In Britain, the police eventually reasserted their authority, and the government managed to defend their history. Meanwhile, in America, the police stepped back considerably, and city after city burned. And now, as a people, we cannot unite around history because the public has been taught a lie about our own history for at least two generations. The monuments that the left is tearing down or placing graffiti on, the protesters keep calling them "your" monuments and do not claim them as their own. Either they are all our monuments, or we are going down the worst possible path, and it's those people that'll lead us there.

That is the path the modern left is taking us down. They are nothing more than today's Jacobeans, and if they gain power, it will end the same: A reign of terror with blood flowing in the streets before consuming itself and ending in America's destruction.

We on the right must refute the sentimental vision of human nature, especially in calls for the abolition of the police. That vision has been shown false by the cruelty and carnage of every revolution it has given rise to. In the anarchical riots in the summer of 2020, we saw the fragility of the social order and the violent aggression that's unleashed when the social order breaks down.

Revolutions naturally tend to empower the most aggressive, ruthless elements, and dislocation and grievances cause the mob to gravitate towards them. That is why Lafayette and Danton fell while Marat and Robespierre took power in France and why in the Russian Revolution Lenin prevailed over Kerensky. As the seeds of a new revolution are spread today by the left, it's crucial for the right to remind the people that revolution devours moderates and empowers violence.

CULTURE WARS

Conservative politics cannot be sustained in a liberal culture. Conservatives cannot achieve any long-term political victory without a cultural victory. That is why the right must fight back against the liberals' war on our culture.

The often-used claim that the right is the side that is waging the culture wars is wrong. By the very definition of words, the left's desire to change cultural values is a "culture war." But one thing we have to ask is, if conservative leaders are unwilling to use power when they have it, do they deserve power at all?

Republican politicians are also idiots. Claiming that any criticism is cancel culture or being silenced, while they complain about it in the Wall Street Journal. There is a grain of truth that people feel like they can't express some things about how they feel, but being criticized is not the same as being canceled.

Reading Dr. Seuss into the congressional record or other amateur stunts like that, that's a sign of a truly decadent political culture. These days, the Republican Party is a victim of its own success and is infantilized because it finds it easy to win in some places. Which is why our politics sucks so much, because it is low stakes.

What we have in our two-party system is timidity. Our elected officials don't have real ambition; they are just satisfied with winning. It's hard to find a politician who is self-possessed and has internal confidence in their own judgement. They're trained on the polls, to look at the reaction on Twitter, listen to the last donor who called, or listen to the think tank experts. We have politicians who are scared to lead. And we think they're going to lead us to victory over the left on anything? I don't think so.

One of the problems with liberalism is the idea that we will inevitably become an ever more perfect society. It's a combination of the trial and error of a pluralistic society and our own rationale that delivers it. As soon as you justify pluralism on those grounds, then liberalism becomes illiberal pretty quickly because whoever disagrees with you about what progress is is almost by definition irrational or nefarious.

This idea allows liberals to give meaning in a meaningless age. Over the last few generations, conservatives have forgotten about the void inside people's souls, and our think tanks and institutions are focused on economics, but that doesn't fill that void. Politics and economics are important, but they don't give humans purpose.

The left is guilty of divorcing social and political organizations from their historical, cultural, and institutional context. It is preposterous to theorize on the basis of a state of nature that never existed and could never have existed. Every member of every generation is born into families, societies, and nations as members of institutions and keepers of traditions. It is the responsibility of every generation to maintain these institutions and traditions in good health.

So, I am left to ask, what are progressives trying to progress beyond? If the principles of our Declaration are permanent because human nature is unchanging, then there can be no progress but only regression away from these principles of equality, inalienable rights, and consent of the governed. Progressives who seek to depart from our founding principles are reactionaries in disguise. They would depart from the ideas that made America the greatest and freest country in human history. Unfortunately for everyone, progressives have firmly taken control of the Democratic Party.

The left relies on resentment, and the right sees the resentment the left is playing with and thinks they can win by playing at a different level. The right should respond with aspiration, doing better for yourself and your loved ones.

◆

The New York Times' 1619 Project and Critical Race Theory are no longer on the extreme left fringes anymore; they are the core of the Democratic Party. The phrase "black lives matter" is relatively uncontroversial, but the implication of those protesting and chanting that phrase is that there are a bunch of people who are terrible racists and don't believe that black lives matter.

Accordingly, progressives are tearing this country apart by demanding it.

What are they wanting? An end to systematic racism, they say. According to Ibram X. Kendi, racism is no longer to be defined as the belief that someone is inferior because of their race. Instead, it is to be defined as the belief that any group differences cannot be attributed to anything other than race. That any system that ends with different outcomes must be racist. That means any system that generates racial inequality must be racist.

And to not be racist, you must be anti-racist. You must tear down any system that allows for different outcomes for different groups. Any obstacle in the pursuit of equality of outcome must be torn down and assumed to be a product of discrimination. You must oppose even institutions that have been considered hallmarks of freedom because they have exacerbated inequalities, or at least failed to rectify those inequalities.

But anti-racism is basically reworked neo-Marxism from the 1960s, as Herbert Marcuse called it "repressive tolerance," or "intolerance against movement from the right and toleration of movements from the left." Now, it has been revived under the banner of race rather than class.

People who neglect the rules of society do not exhibit a higher intelligence, do not promote liberty or equality, but themselves display the standards of ignorance, slavery, and brutality. And the implication is that black people in the United States are under existential threat. That simply isn't the case. The notion out there that police officers are going out there just shooing unarmed black men is not true. The Washington Post itself has reported that the total number of unarmed black men who were shot (not killed) by police in 2019 was 14.

The left also can't have it both ways. The same people who are claiming we need better opportunities in poor minority communities oppose gentrification, but gentrification is bringing more money into those communities. So, if you're going to claim that people are rioting and looting because they're angry about slavery, then you're going to have to explain why other groups in the United States and abroad aren't routinely rioting and looting.

It doesn't have anything to do with slavery; it doesn't even have anything to do with police brutality. It has to do with people taking advantage of a hot situation to get a TV. If anybody suggests that it's justified because America is deeply and endemically racist, it's full of crap. The soft bigotry of low expectations coming from the left is absolutely incredible.

The left is very good at pretending to be sympathetic, the whole virtue signaling issue. It's like pretending to a sympathy that paints you in beautiful, virtuous colors but avoids the cost of it.

The population as a whole needs to understand that the consensus political era is over, at least for now.

Consensus and good-faith negotiation require shared assumptions. The lack of shared assumptions is exactly what the culture war is about. The insistence that the United States is fundamentally good—not perfect, but good—is wholly incompatible with the new left's insistence that it is fundamentally evil. You can't live in a house with a person who wants to burn it down.

CONCLUSION

For the last thirty years, America has had booms and busts in the economy, but the very consistent trend is that most people in the middle of the country haven't done well economically and, more importantly, haven't done well socially either.

There's nothing in our politics about making it easier for people my age and younger to get married, have kids, and live their lives. Those would be actual conservative values instead of this neoliberal nonsense of cutting corporate taxes, deregulating, and bringing in immigrants to keep wages low.

And it's been those predatory economic practices, and a lot of those have been brought on by people in the right wing who bow down and worship the alter of free trade, the free economy, whatever the market can bear, that whole mentality.

That's something we need to get rid of and instead set up an environment that is advantageous to your average hard-working American who wants to build a better life for themselves and their family. It's a moral issue, it's an economic issue, and it's a national security issue.

If your American dream involves being a good husband or wife and a good parent, that dream seems to be disappearing even in the wake of a solid stock market. This crisis in the American dream requires more than the libertarian economics of the right-wing liberal elite, who all too often say that all that is needed to solve the problems in the middle of the country is a supply-side tax cut and a little lecture about personal responsibility. They never consider that maybe it's their policies that are doing more harm than good.

These politicians are different verses to the same tune, and they represent more of the same. Higher taxes for farmers and the workers in the towns, and less and lousier services from the nation. It's all so that these politicians can LARP being freedom fighters from the Revolution instead of actually helping the voters who elected them.

CHAPTER NINE

A WAY FORWARD

Conservatives, in general, are a bit stuck in the past. They remember the Reagan era, and they remember that at that time it was the private sector versus the government. It was the dynamic private sector being held down by regulations and high taxes, and if you could only get the government off its neck, the private sector could create jobs, fuel innovation, create wealth, and drive the country forward.

There are so many good people still caught up in that, for excusable reasons, but that vision and that diagnosis from over 40 years ago is totally out of date. The private sector is not on our side anymore; the private

sector is completely hand-in-glove with the administrative state and the ruling class, and they work together.
And those fights from the Reagan era, the continued
fights over the New Deal, are over now.

They are grounded in the realities of post-Great
Depression America, and we have reached the end of
that. I think we all know that there's not going to be
another Great Society program and we're not going to
abolish Social Security or Medicare. We're not going
to create new programs or new agencies, to give the
problem to experts to administer or plan.

As we face the rise of artificial intelligence or the
rise of China, is the answer going to be more New Deal-
type programs? Is fighting big government the answer?
No, of course not, because those don't make any sense.
We need to solve future problems in a different way.

The ideologies of our current political parties no
longer have the answers to the questions we, as a society,
are facing. A political realignment has or is occurring,
and the more we push back or ignore it, it's going to be
that much more chaotic and dangerous for America.

THE AMERICAN DREAM

The American Dream isn't about, much less a
guarantee of, success. Never has been. It is, however, a
guarantee of a fair chance at success. It promises every
American an equal opportunity to achieve whatever they
desire, no matter the circumstances of their birth. The

government isn't supposed to block your way, and your fellow citizens are supposed to offer you a fair chance to compete and with luck, prevail. Prosperity and economic opportunity are just the most potent byproducts of the American Dream, not its heart.

Looking around today, it's evident that's not how things are going. Almost every aspect of American life seems rigged in favor of the well-connected and wealthy, and that's because, in most cases, it is. Powerful institutions don't play fair or keep their word, while grift and graft flow freely on Wall Street, in law enforcement, advertising, and politics, just to name a few.

Everything about our modern lives is built around the idea that your worth comes from the work you do, and that's wrong. We have to reorient our economic life and policies to incentivize the building of communities and institutions that exist outside of government or a direct check from your workplace. It needs to be about unions, higher wages, and the strength of families. People want to get married, but they can't just afford to. Marriage is essentially a luxury good now.

How do we raise wages so that a middle-class family can live a middle-class life on a single income? Lose foreign competition. Make it profitable to build manufacturing here again, which will mean excluding some imports.

In the spring of 2020, we found out that America really couldn't produce N-95 masks or ventilators in our country. That we didn't make antibiotics or even the precursor chemicals for antibiotics, so even if we wanted to make the drugs, we couldn't. The answer to that is that we need to legally require that some things have to be made in the United States. We need to be self-sufficient in food, energy, and healthcare products. We need to be secure and not dependent on China, India, or any other nation when it comes to those things.

The long-time trope is that the American Dream is owning a house with a white picket fence and a well-manicured yard, and that's not exactly wrong. But we have to do whatever it takes to build up our population and make it easier for people to live near their families and in the communities they want to, and not be forced to move out of the state to be able to live a middle-class life. Owning a home gives people pride and human dignity. It helps citizens buy into their society and community, allowing people to plant roots and start families.

Many millennials aren't able to form families like Gen-X or Baby Boomers. We aren't buying homes; we aren't attaining the level of wealth previous generations had at our age, and we aren't having as many kids as we want to have. There are many reasons for this, of course, but the fact is that the middle class is dying. Some are filtering up, but most are moving down, and their lives are becoming more precarious.

We have a generation of college-educated, debt-saddled, hardworking Americans who just want to get a job, ply their trade, and get out of debt. Still, they're unable to do that because it's a rigged system. Now we have a generation that can't get married. If they do get married and want to have kids, now there's this issue of how we will pay for childcare.

They can't own a home. Homeownership has become this unattainable thing for an entire generation, so the American Dream has been stomped all over. And it's been predatory economic practices, and many of those have been brought on by people in the right-wing who bow down and worship the altar of free trade, the free economy, whatever the market can bear, that whole mentality.

There are apocryphal stories from realtors that at least half of first-time homebuyers are receiving gifts from parents or grandparents so they can put down the down payment, otherwise they don't have a chance. The median home price in America has risen 19% in the last year to an average price of $341,600 for a home. A normal down payment for that home is $68,200, which is a standard deviation above the average family yearly income. How can people save up this kind of money?

I really don't think that people in power understand how screwed over Millennials are. Yes, previous generations had their own struggles and difficulties to handle, and if that is all that was happening, I wouldn't be writing this. The difference in this case is that for many in this cohort, the American dream is dead. What we're seeing is that the working- and middle-classes have no chance in hell right now.

That's something we need to get rid of and set up an environment that is advantageous to your average hard-working American who wants to build a better life for themselves and their family. It's a moral issue, an economic issue, and a national security issue. And before any libertarian says it, I don't want to hear it. We shouldn't have to uproot ourselves and our families to live a decent life. Or make it that if we refuse to move, we will die or get hooked on opioids or meth.

In this issue, the right and left have different complaints that really are the same complaint coming from different directions. Whether it's because of global competition, or because there are people in charge of the system, or because they don't like people like you or me, they all seem to agree that the system doesn't work. Institutions don't do what they're supposed to do, they don't work the way they work on paper, and there's a set of rules we publish and a real set of rules for what's actually happening. The game is rigged; ordinary people like me no longer have a chance. The system no longer works for ordinary people. I can work hard and play by the rules, but I'm not playing on a level playing field anymore.

Conservatism must seek to restore the American Dream of social equality. In a democracy, we're social equals. We're not all economic equals; we don't have the same abilities, but we're all socially equal and of the same dignity, and we're all entitled to a fair shot at our dreams. And if we work hard and get a little lucky, everyone should have an equal chance at a decent life. No one should be cutting in line. We have to make the system work the way we say it works. Get rid of corruption, make institutions live up to their stated values, and restore the promise of the American Dream.

RENEWED CONSERVATISM

As I have grown and matured in my political life, I find myself drawn towards the early 20th century Republican Party platform of trade protection, immigration restriction, and foreign policy restraint. In essence, the need to do what is good for the average American family. We can do this through an ambitious economic policy, traditional social conservatism, and a restrained foreign policy.

To me, an ambitious nationalist economic policy would comprise of tariff-based protections for vital industries, a reformed national financial system and central bank, restricted immigration, and national infrastructure projects to rebuild our nation. A traditional social conservatism brings expressly pro-family policies that encourage marriage and raising children and against the cultural leftism that wants to destroy our history and heritage. And a restrained foreign policy would be one where America doesn't meddle in every single thing that happens in other nations, where we are not the world's beat cop, going in with our military whenever our sensibilities are out of place, acting like the world's imperial power.

A crucial part of this renewed conservatism is nationalism. Contrary to the howling of the left and Conservative Inc., nationalism is nothing more than the love of one's own people, institutions, and culture, and the belief that an individual can make his most significant contributions to humanity by contributing to his nation.

In his *Reflections on the Revolution in France*, the father of modern conservatism, Edmund Burke, wrote, "To be attached to the subdivision, to love the little platoon we belong to in society, is the first principle (the germ as it were) of public affections It is the first link in the series by which we proceed towards a love to our country, and to mankind." So, in my mind, it is not wrong to be a nationalist; it's a good thing.

The right must wield political power when it is given to us, not abdicate our responsibilities out of some delusional thought that if we don't use that power, it will go away on its own. The right must return to its foundational principles and should look to other right-wing movements across the globe to forge a new path forward because not many people know how to be conservative these days. They think it means to just be against whatever the left does or is some strange absolute commitment to the free market. That is absolutely wrong.

The right-wing liberal policies of Conservative Inc., of free-market fundamentalism, free trade, individualism, and tax cuts and deregulation always being the answer, no longer work and need to go away. Real conservatives value strong families, strong communities, and strong nations over GDP growth and cheap prices. The country you see today is the result of a conservative movement that cared for nothing but small government and tax cuts. We need a return to actual conservatism: faith first, then family, and duty to our country. Not this over-indulgent, selfish individualist libertarianism.

Mainstream conservatives ought to stop pretending that immoral companies like Facebook, Nike, Apple, Amazon, etc., are the best that capitalism has to offer. These companies hate conservatives and want us un-personed. They're not your friends. The debate between socialism and reckless, unsustainable right-wing liberal consumerism is a false dichotomy. We can create a healthy, sustainable, nationalist market economy that works for American families.

Free markets are simply a tool to allocate resources and structure economies effectively. They do not need to be protected absolutely. America is a country with an economy, not an economy with a country attached on. At the same time, government budgets must be rewritten from scratch.

We have to figure out what we want the government to do and go from there. Taxation needs to be simplified, lowered, and exemptions eliminated. We should have a national policy of advancing technological innovation in the fields of astrophysics, fusion energy production, applied physics, and more that are not yet developed.

The right needs to return to traditional social conservatism to rebuild and grow families and communities that can turn away from the woke culture of the left. The great liberalization that has occurred since World War II has eroded our morals, communities, families and is now going after our very history. The birth rate has fallen, marriages have slowed, and divorces are still high. Importing immigrants is not the answer to falling birth rates. We need to create policies that encourage marriage and children.

We have to reject the selfish individualism of right-wing liberals and, in order to rebuild our communities, embrace our obligations towards not just our neighbors but also to those that came before and those yet to come.

The final core piece of a renewed conservatism is a restrained foreign policy that, militarily, is not so involved in every squabble on this planet but ready to defend our nation without hesitation. Despite what is portrayed, the American military does have limitations. We need to be disabused of the notion that the military is still competent, that it's immune from the rot that's infected every other institution in our government. Our operations in Iraq and Afghanistan have shown us otherwise.

At the same time, we need to remain militarily strong and develop advanced technologies to beat back future adversaries such as China. On a diplomatic level,

America needs to eliminate our imperial strategy of imposing a liberal western democracy on every tribe and nation on this planet. We are not responsible for what happens in other sovereign nations. We should wish them the best, but if they want freedom and liberty, then it is their responsibility to fight for it.

THE PARTY

I'm not entirely convinced the Republican Party is up to the task anymore – but I'm not sure if the answer is a new party or reforge the old one. The Republican Party of today is stuck on the same platform and issues, when we need to throw away the archaic messages of New Deal liberalism or fighting big government and instead construct a completely different message from scratch.

Whether it's a new party or refreshing an old one, we need a new party ideology that can create a new agenda that actually speaks to the problems that keep Americans up at night. This message built around the American Dream would recognize the fears most Americans share about their future. It would explain what exactly is broken in America and propose what must be done to fix it. And provide a framework to build a positive agenda of ideas to make the future better.

We need an ideology dedicated to preserving the nation's virtues for the benefit of ordinary Americans. That would cherish the values of traditional America—

patriotism, hard work, Judeo-Christian values, and traditional cultural conservatism—and fight against the power of both economic and cultural elites pushing changes harmful to the people. Celebrate the virtue of ordinary working people. Denigrate out-of-touch elites living in rich communities as dangerous, others more loyal to the global elite than working Americans.

Can the Republican Party change?

I'm afraid that the party is unwilling to do that. If we can capture it and transform the party as William Jennings Bryan transformed the Democratic Party in 1896, that would be terrific and the best option. The only alternative is to create a new party separate from the current GOP.

If building a new party is the way forward, then the first rule we have to follow is that it can't be a futile attempt to recreate a party that's dying, or already dead. A new party has to break with orthodoxy and think fresh. Many former Republicans need to understand this point in particular. The old 20th-century Republican Party isn't dying because someone took it away from them. It's dying because it was an anachronism even before Donald Trump climbed out of a reality-TV set to embarrass it. Its coalition is no longer united around a common purpose, and its ideology lacks the tools needed to navigate a changed America. It can no longer hold its old coalition together around the dead issues of the past.

It's not uncommon to see the displaced leaders of a dying party, dismayed at the shattering of the institution around which they built careers, form a splinter party to restore a status quo. Stubborn holdouts once tried to rebuild both the Federalists and the Whigs years after they were all but buried. Democratic leaders, booted out of their party by William Jennings Bryan, tried to challenge him by mounting a new party under their old ideas and failed. This strategy has never, ever worked.

A new party can't succeed by trying to restore the ideologies of the past because reality has left those ideologies in the dustbin of history. If your idea of a new party is reanimating the 20th-century Republicans or Democrats, you will fail. That's not building a new party; it's trying to resurrect a dead one. Zombies aren't real, and it's a good thing they're not. A new party needs to think about problems in a fresh way, attracting a new coalition that pulls across old divides.

Next, we would start by building the intellectual infrastructure to develop new ideas. We need to fill the role that institutions like The New Republic, which helped develop the ideas that united the Progressive Movement, or FDR's "brain trust," which turned an economic crisis into the foundation of the ideology that united Democrats for generations, or National Review, which turned the feuding factions opposed to the New Deal into a coherent group of conservatives, played in earlier times. Find great minds, free them to think unchained to orthodoxy, and ask them to see the world with fresh eyes. When aging political professionals think about forming a new party, they immediately want to know what policy agenda the party will support and the demographic groups it can attract. That's backwards.

You can't unite 51 percent of Americans under one of the two major parties and then sustain that alliance for decades around a collection of unrelated programs, policy preferences, or talking points. The only way to unite hundreds of millions of diverse people for long enough to matter is with a sweeping idea addressing the big problem that a consensus believes is endangering the integrity of the commonweal.

Each discrete political era in America is essentially defined by a great debate around which all political energies revolve. Each party represents a theory about what has gone wrong and the correct approach to fixing it.

Stop thinking about the policies you want your new party to support. Definitely give up hope of founding a party around the policies you supported in the 20th-century. Start thinking about the big new problem that begs a solution and your fresh approach to solving it. That's how to unite hundreds of millions of Americans in a common cause, even people who disagree about many things and, at least at first, don't trust one another all that much.

The third rule for building a new party is that it has to have a positive message about the future. Stop thinking about what you don't want and start thinking about what you do want. You can't unite a majority coalition for decades of campaigns around stopping someone else's bad ideas or a politician you dislike. The Whigs formed in opposition to Andrew Jackson, but they didn't stop there: They developed an avowedly Hamiltonian agenda for a strong, unified, progressing nation. Yet again, a new party needs to give people a common plan to make tomorrow's world better. It doesn't hurt at first for a new party to coalesce around a common perception of danger, but you need to tell a story with a happy ending for those willing to work together for it.

Now, it's true: opposition parties built around stopping supposedly bad ideas do exist. That kind of opposition will arise to one extent or another, because major change always gores someone's ox more than it promises to feed others. Can an agglomeration like that persist, let alone prevail, in American politics today? I doubt it. Deep down we remain an intrepid, forward-looking people. We are still pioneers of a sort.

What's beyond dispute, then, is that opposition isn't enough. A new party must be positive, forward-thinking, and able to spark fresh solutions.

The fourth rule for building a new party is that you actually have to build one from the bottom up, not just run one campaign. You can't establish a new ideology by winning the White House in a personality-based presidential campaign. A new party has to start from the ground up around a popular movement. Even if you capture people's attention around a leader, that leader has to stand for a genuine movement rising from the people. In short, in a very real sense, a new political party has to stand on the shoulders of a social movement. The model is Lincoln's Republicans, not the one-man crusade of Ross Perot.

So, don't start with political consultants who are experts at winning individual elections. Start with local infrastructure, organization, and ideas. Build a presence in each state. Open offices, sponsor fairs, concerts, debates, clubs, and social-action groups. Build networks that reach into every corner of America to create supporters and to discover leaders. Start by electing like-minded people to state houses, Congress, and governorships. Build a national party not around winning just one election, but around advancing your ideas.

Then compete in the next midterm elections. Don't start with the presidency. Look to Congress and the state houses with a slate of new candidates drawing from both old parties. Find some folks with no links to the prior era's politics at all. Avoid politicians and longtime activists looking to extend their careers or hitchhike old ideas onto new vehicles. Set out to win just twenty seats in the House of Representatives, two Senate seats, and a governorship. Do that and people have to take you seriously.

Finally, once all that is achieved, look for a President. Once you have the right big radioactive idea, with a fetching narrative to match and a new group of leaders unchained from the past, you can campaign for the presidency. Don't look to some rich mogul because he's willing to finance his own campaign. Don't look to some aging senator. Look for the next Lincoln, someone with a record of caring about the country, someone with manifest passion and potential greatness whom the previous era overlooked.

Campaign around the American Dream. Of course, you need a soaring message, not something out of a policy wonk's report. You need to unite hundreds of millions of Americans around a vision in which our greatest crisis yields to new hope.

Think about FDR's New Deal brain trust. FDR didn't just try to slap a few new policies onto the old Democratic agenda. He assembled a group of experts, scholars, and policy minds and tasked them with developing a new agenda to address the crisis of the Great Depression. The group drew across old partisan lines, and its proposals were novel. Instead of trying to patch over his old party agenda or buying off groups of voters with carefully pitched policies, he sought to identify and solve the most difficult and unfamiliar problems stalking the nation.

Our new party has to do the same thing. It has to develop a new agenda relevant to our onrushing 21st-century world. It has to be forward-looking, which is the best way to transcend the vicious disagreements of the present to create new coalition bonds. What people differ about from the past cannot be allowed to swallow what they agree about looking to the future. Whatever big ideas your new party proposes should surprise us, because it will be experimenting and innovating to solve real problems that so far nobody has even properly named.

CLOSING THOUGHTS

Conservatism, as Edmund Burke said, is not so much an ideology as a philosophy of life. But when we have modern day Jacobeans tearing at the foundations of the Anglo-American world, we must take them head on in a true reactionary spirit and fight back.

But instead, we're pretending to know a lot of things about things we just don't know enough about. We're pretending we don't know things that everyone knew yesterday.

The presumption of modernity is that we are better than people in the past because we know more than people in the past, but we are just as vulnerable to crowd madness and strange phenomena. The present is better than the past. But in order for the future to be better still, we must preserve the ways that the present has become better than the past. And the progressives and neo-Marxists don't want to do that. Conservatism is about recovery and restoration; it's about love of what we have.

Contrasting with libertarians, conservatives upholds the value of individuals, but it's not just all about them. We don't see individuals out there just doing their own thing, but rather as individuals plugged into a bigger picture, through our institutions. We need something beyond ourselves to focus on. A community.

In my own state of Nebraska, the current Republican administration is mostly fine on fiscal and social policy, but it lacks a conservative soul. Conservatism is not just about lower taxes or limiting government regulations. Yes, we do these to uphold natural law and to provide good governance, but by focusing on just that, you miss beauty and the sublime, as Burke put it.

◆

Conservative Inc. and the Republican Party elites want you to think there's something wrong with being a populist or a nationalist. That there's something wrong with believing in hierarchy and order. But there's nothing wrong with any of those things.

They want to return to the days of talking about limited government and tax cuts being enough for voters. And it isn't. There isn't any going back to what we had before. We need to deal with today's realities and go from there.

Voters on the right don't care as much about cutting entitlements or cutting taxes—they're more socially conservative than economically libertarian, and there has been a fundamental misunderstanding on the right over the last 20 years that Republican leaders cared about us. They don't.

I keep repeating this, but it's to drive the point home: the goal of the right should not be to achieve tax cuts or deregulation. It should be to rebuild American families, restore American sovereignty, and revitalize American culture.

I care less about individualism's placing the individual above society than I care about having families and communities grow and flourish. Because that is the future of our society, and if we let them fall, then we're all screwed.

Government power isn't something to be afraid of, we can use it for conservative ends. I'm not for creating government programs for the sake of creating government programs, but I want the government to put guardrails in place and referee things, so corporations do not take advantage of or steamroll over the average person. A lot of us have gotten fed up with the idea that corporations should have all the power and CEOs should write the rules for the rest of us. The thing is, we, as individuals, don't have the power to keep corporations in check; the government does. Corporate power needs to be kept in check against its authoritarian tendencies just like the government.

Cutting taxes for corporations and deregulation, those are donor-class issues. You don't win elections on those. There's no constituency for that neoliberal economics, and even the biggest proponents of neoliberalism in the Republican Party admit that. Politicians have bought into this idea that taxes are bad, regulations are bad, and we just need to unleash the animal forces of the market. That's a load of garbage.

The giant cosmic lie is that if we just let money flow where it wants to (which really means where the donor class wants it to), wealth will magically trickle down through the economy, something that has happened exactly zero times.

I believe this and am willing to have this fight because a lot of what ordinary people want is not to have to think about public policy. They want to live a life where they feel supported by their family and their community, and there isn't a lot of noisy bullshit fighting around them all the time. And I want to give them that.

That is why we must re-industrialize America. That is why we need to have more balanced trade, reduce our debt, and make businesses that have left return to America. That is why we need to protect our technological innovations and stop giving them away to foreign adversaries. That is why we must help small businesses thrive and be passed on from generation to generation.

That is why we need to preserve our culture and our nation. That is why we need to restore our public-school system, its excellence, and stop exposing our children to the experiments of crazy gender theorists and the radical progressive left. That is why we need to reclaim our sovereignty, which was given away to the globalist elite, who have stripped America of our ability to produce anything meaningful in the name of free-markets.

Yes, we must give power back to the people; take it back from minorities that keep imposing tyranny on the majority and from judges who substitute their legal power for the government of the people, by the people, for the people. For decades, the left and the right have led us down this deadly path of decline and decadence. Left and right, they have lied to you. They have hidden the gravity of our decline. But no more.

We need a president with the will to break up the quasi-monopolies that run huge segments of our country. We shouldn't be okay with Walmart or Dollar General running mom-and-pop shops out of business or other large corporations shipping jobs overseas. We should appropriately respond to their malfeasance by using the power of the state to push back. We should also demand that state governments stop investing their pensions with woke investment firms that push critical race theory "training."

That's how you protect small businesses and the working class by punishing the institutions that gobble up significant portions of the market and drive down wages by importing foreign labor and shipping jobs overseas. You don't attack someone who loses $42,000 a year in passive income.

In short, conservatism as both a way of life and a political movement is in crisis. And there has been none of the self-reflection, humility, or behavioral changes that should accompany the obvious failures that have led us to this point. Instead, we get furious justifications, condescending dismissals, and navel-gazing about the economic theories of comparative advantage. Or worse, blanket apathy.

After years of our conservative institutions and leaders telling us "they have it in hand," these last few years has unmasked their claim as mistaken at best, and outright lies at worst. Apathy and self-righteous justifications will be met with apathy and disgust by the voters in November. The only thing that can begin to bring this movement back to relevance is an intellectually humble reevaluation of how D.C. conservatism lost its ability to create a clear and coherent way forward for those who seek its leadership. But there is precious little time for the ship to begin righting itself.

That work must begin in earnest—and begin immediately.

www.ingramcontent.com/pod-product-compliance
Lightning Source LLC
Chambersburg PA
CBHW051728260326
41914CB00040B/2016/J